THE
MODERN WITCH'S
BOOK OF
MANIFESTATION

THE MODERN WITCH'S BOOK OF MANIFESTATION

SARAH BARTLETT

First published in Great Britain in 2023 by Yellow Kite
An imprint of Hodder & Stoughton
An Hachette UK company

The authorised representative in the EEA is Hachette Ireland, 8 Castlecourt
Centre, Dublin 15, D15 XTP3, Ireland (email: info@hbgi.ie)

3

A CIP catalogue record for this title is available from the British Library

Hardback ISBN 978 1 39972 229 2
Ebook ISBN 978 1 399 72230 8

Typeset in Nocturne Serif by Hewer Text UK Ltd, Edinburgh
Printed and bound in Great Britain by Clays Ltd, Elcograf S.p.A.

Hodder & Stoughton policy is to use papers that are natural, renewable
and recyclable products and made from wood grown in sustainable
forests. The logging and manufacturing processes are expected to
conform to the environmental regulations of the country of origin.

Yellow Kite
Hodder & Stoughton Ltd
Carmelite House
50 Victoria Embankment
London EC4Y 0DZ

www.yellowkitebooks.co.uk

To all my family and friends, and for being who you are.

Contents

Introduction

That which is below is like that which is above and
that which is above is like that which is below.
Sir Isaac Newton, English physicist,
astronomer and alchemist

There is nothing spooky about being a modern witch. In fact, you already are one. Each and every one of us has an essential connection to the magic of the universe, simply by virtue of being born on this planet.

The modern witch is self-empowered, knows what they truly desire and trusts in their ability to achieve it. They are also innately gifted.

Perhaps as a child you had 'imaginary friends' or spirit guides. You may have read messages at times in shapes, signs, symbols and patterns, or understood nature's ways and sensed the invisible world that lies within and beyond. You may not remember this now, but you did, and you will again. Because it's time to reclaim your power by accessing this inner gift.

Manifestation (the fulfilment or realisation of a goal or intention) is intrinsic to the art of witchcraft – for all magic is about the intention to make something happen. And you *do* want something to happen . . . or you would not be reading this book!

When I was about nine years old, I entered a fancy-dress competition. I insisted on dressing up as a witch, so my mother bought lengths of black crepe paper, which she stapled together for a cloak, we crafted a cardboard box into a cone-shaped pointed hat and borrowed a long-handled brush, which we dressed with brown paper strips to resemble a broomstick. I waved my magic wand (a paintbrush), absolutely sure that I could work magic and win the competition. My wish came true, and I manifested my first dream as a little crepe-papered witch who won first prize.

I'm sure there's something in your life you want to manifest and make real. Maybe a desire for new romance, a longing for reconnection with nature, a career goal or simply a greater awareness of your qualities, manifesting self-belief and confidence? Drawing on your inner witch (and I will tell you how to do this, using traditional lore, contemporary ingredients and truly believing in your intentions) will help you to achieve these things and more.

Belief fuels intention and is fundamental to making something happen – my belief that I would win that first prize is just one example. Words in themselves also have power, and the more you believe in your desire, and the more you 'spell' it out – and I mean 'magically' spell and speak it here – the more it will be channelled to the universe and the more likely it is that it will manifest in your life.

In Part One, you will use rituals to encourage your connection to your inner witch, while in Part Two you will use spells to help you manifest your dreams. For the purposes of this book, there is a subtle distinction between a ritual and a spell: a ritual is a series of prescribed steps carried out in sequence to achieve a particular result, whereas a spell involves the use of specific words, gestures and ingredients that draw on magical power to fulfil your intention.

Some of the spells and rituals involve plants and substances that some people might be allergic to, so take care not to use anything that might cause you problems and use a substitute instead. And please take care when using candles and smudge sticks. Make sure that they do not come into contact with anything that might catch fire. Ensuring that they are safely and thoroughly snuffed out is as important to the spells and rituals as lighting them.

So now, with a little help from outer magic and your inner witch, it's time to transform your wishes and desires into reality. Read on to learn how to tap into your natural connection to the magic of the universe – to rediscover and reclaim your power and start to realise your dreams. By embracing and loving yourself, and trusting in your affinity with the universe, you can draw on your inner witch to manifest all that you truly seek.

PART ONE

Your Modern Witchcraft Primer

This part of the book gives you an overview of witchcraft and manifestation and what they are all about. There is also a brief introduction to the different types of witches and you will read about the history of witchcraft and Wicca, too, and how to connect to your inner witch using ritual work. Plus, there are chapters detailing how to work with ingredients such as crystals, botanicals, deities, the planets and symbolic empowerments. So let's get to work.

CHAPTER ONE

The World of Witchcraft

*Whatever you can do, or dream you
can, begin it. Boldness has genius, power
and magic in it. Begin it now.*
**Johann Wolfgang von Goethe, German
poet, playwright and scientist**

Witchcraft, quite simply, is the practice of harnessing the inherent magic of the universe for the purpose of achieving a desired outcome. This magic is an energy, if you like, thought to permeate and shape the universe, and is a divine or animating force.

The 'craft' of the witch has been around for thousands of years and, according to different worldwide traditions, has been regarded with favour and scorn, but, mostly, fear – especially during the patriarchal witch-hunts of mediaeval Europe. However, in most ancient indigenous cultures and traditions, witchcraft was considered a beneficial way to heal, overcome fear and loss, promote strength, attract love and manifest desires.

These days, in modern witchcraft, various types of magic are used, including sympathetic, natural, ceremonial and folk. Here's a brief guide:

* **Sympathetic magic** uses objects or symbols that represent your desired outcome. For example, placing gold coins, gold ribbons or a piece of gold in your hall-way will attract more 'gold' into your life. This is the most common and simple way to help manifest your goals.

* **Natural magic** works with everything in nature to focus and amplify the energy of your desire – such as herbs, other botanicals, symbols, planets, deities (the gods and goddesses who embody all facets of the natural world), nature's cycles and crystals.

* **Ceremonial magic** (or 'high magic', as it's sometimes called) uses particular rituals and elaborate interaction with a deity, spiritual entity and/or a specific belief system. It often involves complex spell work, secret codes or formulae and association with a coven (a group of witches) or secret group.

* **Folk magic** is a mixture of sympathetic and natural magic, but often includes local lore, superstitions and beliefs.

The modern witch uses a combination of sympathetic, natural and folk magic, along with a heavy dose of self-belief, care and good intentions for all. In fact, magic has always been a way of harnessing the energies of nature – a collaboration between your individual desires, your inner witch and the outer world. It is only by connecting with the universe in this way that manifesting your goals will truly happen.

Witches Through History

In Paleolithic times, protective talismans and symbols were carved into rocks to call on spirits, protect crops, aid hunting, invoke fertility and banish evil influences or rival clans. In Babylonian, Egyptian, Greek and Roman civilisations, deities were associated with the planets and their corresponding qualities and powers. For example, the Greek goddesses Selene and Hecate were identified with the moon, while Aphrodite, the goddess of love, was identified with Venus. By working with talismans, symbols and corresponding energies relating to the deities, the ancients believed they could make changes in their own and other people's lives.

Some magicians and sorcerers began to write down their spells in grimoires (texts of recipes, ingredients, charms and talismans) and established their own traditions and codes. Two extant magic texts, the Papyrus of Ani (*c.* 1250BCE), also known as the *Book of the Dead*, and the Greek Magical Papyri (*c.* 200BCE–400CE) are collections of parchment fragments filled with wondrous and some quite ghastly spells. (Both are available in translation if you are curious.) Spells in these texts include remedies for impotence, curse tablets, love charms and amulets.

By the Middle Ages, the average 'witch' was usually someone in the local community who knew a lot about healing herbs, potions, love elixirs, protective amulets and beneficial talismans. However, in Europe, the Protestant and Catholic Churches, fearful of subversive pagan belief systems circulating among ordinary folk, and in an attempt to attract new followers, prompted a witch-hunt frenzy, resulting in the persecution and murder of thousands of innocent people. Anyone dabbling in matters of the occult had little choice but to face the inquisition and the stake or go 'underground'.

By the end of the nineteenth century, a renewed interest in spirituality in England had brought 'magic' to life again. An occult group known as the Hermetic Order of the Golden Dawn revived Hermetic esotericism (an ancient philosophical system based on the teachings of the legendary Hermes Trismegistus). One of the order's members – the notorious, flamboyant and controversial occultist, writer and mountaineer Aleister Crowley – founded his own alternative religion. Known as 'Thelema', its core tenet, 'Do what thou wilt', included ceremonial sex and drug-induced 'magick' for initiates. Crowley was an unconventional and defiant character, who, irrespective of his questionable beliefs, had a huge influence on twentieth-century Western magic (not least on the so-called 'Father of Wicca', Gerald Gardner – see p. 9).

Modern Witchcraft

Nowadays, witchcraft is about helping ourselves and others in a positive, healing or compassionate way; it is not about controlling or denying free will.

The modern witch doesn't attempt to manipulate universal forces, but asks for help from them. They give blessings and gratitude to the universe, and draw on their own self-belief, realising they are part of the whole, and that what they put out to the universe or ask for help with is for the good of everything and everyone else, too.

A modern witch of any kind respects, honours and connects to nature, knowing that the magic of the universe flows through all things. Most witches may not follow set rituals, but simply draw on their intuitive integrity to take control of their lives, to manifest their desires and to heal, nurture and restore goodness to the world around them.

Which witch?

Let's get this straight: you don't have to have had a grandmother who was a witch or other ancestors who 'dabbled' in witchcraft. (Although, if any of us goes back three, four or more generations, there is bound to be someone in our family history who knew something about plants, flowers, herbs and healing recipes.)

Wicca is often used as a general term for witchcraft. But Wicca is a belief system in its own right, and doesn't necessarily involve practising magic – although it can (for more on this see p. 9). Other terms, such as 'eclectic witches', 'hedge witches' and 'green witches', are also bandied about – so which witch do *you* identify with, if any?

The solitary witch

When practising witchcraft, you might decide to make a commitment to an established group (such as the various branches of Wicca) or prefer to practise alone. As the name suggests, a solitary witch makes their own rules, chooses their own times to perform their craft and isn't reliant on participation in a ritualistic group.

THE ECLECTIC WITCH

This is a solitary witch who draws on a wide variety of witchcraft methods and neopagan beliefs to manifest their goals.

THE GREEN WITCH

The 'green' witch is, again, a solitary witch, but one who works primarily with natural magic (see p. 4).

THE HEDGE WITCH

Before the rise of women's equality in Western patriarchal societies, it was assumed that a woman took on the role of wife, mother, nurse, cook and cleaner. But in choosing the contents of their stews, they no doubt discovered invaluable information about how to use ingredients for other purposes. These women were probably what we might now call hedge witches.

Hedge witchcraft is practised by solitary witches, and involves working with and cultivating plants, herbs and other natural ingredients to create spells for healing purposes. The name 'hedge witch' apparently originates in Irish folklore and was usually applied to a wise woman of the village who understood how to use herbs, forage for fungi and concoct healing potions from local plants. She lived on the edge of the village by the countryside (hence the hedgerow association), forming a boundary between the heart of the community and the wild beyond. She knew everything that was going on in her patch, and was often counsellor, diviner, cunning woman, match-maker and more.

WICCA

The principles and beliefs behind Wicca may appeal to you more if you like a stabilising and unified element in your practice. In Wicca you can be as invisible or as transparent as you desire, and you may feel more comfortable practising within traditional guidelines.

First developed in mid-twentieth-century Britain, Wicca is a neopagan belief system (as mentioned, you don't have to prac-tise witchcraft to be a Wiccan). Anthropologist, folklorist and author Margaret Murray (1863–1963) was interested in pre-Christian pagan religion, and believed it was still being practised in secret covens (she suggested groups of usually thirteen members) all across Europe. The British author and occultist Gerald Gardner (1884–1964) was fascinated by all things pagan, too, and after reading Murray's work he came across a British coven called the New Forest Group (based in the south of England). In the 1940s, intent on making sure the ancient craft

THE MODERN WITCH'S BOOK OF MANIFESTATION

survived, he developed his new 'religion' by forming his Bricket Wood Coven and calling his initiates 'the Wica', an old Anglo-Saxon word for sorcerers and wise crafters. However, although he never labelled his religion 'Wicca', Gardner's collaborators soon developed his ideas, and the movement spread to the States and beyond. Since the 1950s and 60s, Wicca has become an established neopagan religion with many offshoots throughout the world.

The core belief of all Wicca is that the divine flows through all things. The essential and fundamental focus is to worship the Earth, honour natural cycles, live by the seasons, follow and give thanks at the sabbats (festive breaks) and esbats (lunar phases) and live by the movement of the sun and moon throughout the year. Wiccans also work with deities, nature's mysteries, the planets and animal spirits with the intention of connecting to the divine or universal source.

Of course, you can ditch the witch labels altogether and just be you – someone who uses witchy knowledge to make their dreams come true.

ANIMISM

Whatever kind of witch you want to call yourself (or perhaps you prefer no label at all), it is important that you believe in the unifying force of all 'witchy ways'. Also known as animism, this is simply the belief that a divine force – also known as 'ch'i' (in Taoist philosophy) or 'prana' (in Sanskrit) – flows through all things, uniting everything as one. This force flows through the

Earth and cosmos, all of nature – trees, flowers, animals, rocks, the sea, the weather, the planets, humanity, the constellations – and animates every living thing with its own unique essence or quality.

The concept of animism is fundamental to practising any kind of witchcraft. Whether you believe in the gods and spirits or prefer to just call on the universe, manifesting your goals needs to be fuelled not only by nature's apparent powers, but its invisible ones, too.

The law of attraction

No modern-day witch would be a witch if they didn't draw on the law of attraction. In fact, the concept has been postulated in philosophical and occult circles alike since ancient times.

The ancient esoteric viewpoint is 'As above, so below' or, 'What we are is what we attract.' In other words, whatever true intention is fired out into the universe, we attract this quality back into our lives.

In practice, this means, for example, that self-love generates more loving energy around you; or an utter belief in your own talent will mean that mentors and possible investors have utter belief in it, too; and if you believe in your own talents and have an authentic passion for success, then the universe will bring you success. But if you're feeling negative about yourself, the world will send negativity back at you. In essence, the law of attraction says that you get what you think about and therefore your thoughts determine your destiny. So if you think,

11

believe and act positively, you will receive positive energy in return.

There are currently various popular ways to manifest, which don't in themselves claim to use witchcraft (although some might say they are pretty witchy). For example, there is the 369 method (see p. 231); and another is a visualisation technique where you imagine whispering a positive intention into the ear of someone you want to help you achieve your goal (see p. 232). These methods use two of the most powerful practices in witchcraft: the power of numbers (see p. 99) and the power of your imagination. I have woven them into some of the spells in Part Two to amplify their power.

Witchcraft Works

Witchcraft has been around for thousands of years, and it works because it draws directly on the hidden powers of the universe.

But witchcraft isn't just writing down or saying a spell; it also takes a lot of confidence, a true passion for what you are hoping to manifest and, most of all, self-belief.

The key to manifesting your dreams isn't so much about just willing them to happen or mere visualisation – although these do have a place. It will *only* work with 100-per-cent self-belief and acceptance that the invisible power of the universe flows through you, protecting and nurturing your dream or goal. And the great news is that with true intention, belief, goodness and gratitude, you can start to make things happen.

*   *   *

Now that you know more about what witchcraft is – and isn't – the following chapters will give you not only a wide range of traditional 'tools' and 'ingredients' to use in your spell work, but also techniques for acquiring more confidence and belief in your modern-witchcraft practice.

CHAPTER TWO

The Witch's Toolbox

*Nature . . . will hang the night with stars so that I may
walk abroad in the darkness without stumbling, and
send word the wind over my footprints so that none
may track me to my hurt: she will cleanse me in great
waters, and with bitter herbs make me whole.*
Oscar Wilde, Irish playwright, poet and novelist

To reinforce your deepest desires requires a little help
from the world around you. As previously mentioned,
everything in nature is animated and alive with the
divine, and so the more we ask for help from those
elements around us, the more likely it is that we'll be in
contact with the source of this divine energy itself. You
don't have to surround yourself with broomsticks and
cauldrons to perform manifesting magic (although you
can if you like), but every witch needs a little help from the
natural world to capture the magic power inherent in all
things.

The modern witch's toolbox includes symbols, colour,
stones, crystals, candles, botanical elements, essential oils

THE MODERN WITCH'S BOOK OF MANIFESTATION

and the odd potion to help achieve their desires. Assemble a simple toolkit from each of the categories below; these are the basic building blocks of any manifesting spell, but if you can't get hold of them all, you can always improvise, referring to the Correspondence List on p. 275.

Candles

A word of warning: please take safety precautions when lighting or extinguishing candles and when working with them while they are alight.

Many spells call for candles because they are directly associated with Fire energy. Fire energy burns through the obstacles that might cross your well-intended path and lights up your intention with its magical spark. Candles also 'fire off' your intention to the universe and, of course, their flames symbolise the burning desire of your requests, while blowing them out seals your intention to the universe and ends the spell.

So when a spell calls for lit candles, proceed with caution and use only in a safe place, where you know they won't get knocked over or set fire to your clothes or anything else near by.

Tea lights are probably the safest candles to use. And if you place them in little saucers or cups, all the better. Long, tapered candles can be used unlit or, if lit, only on a stable surface and in sturdy holders. If you really don't want to light your candle, you can imagine it lit instead, but you have to really be able to visualise this and hold the image for as long as the spell takes. Or, if you prefer, you could use 'candles' with fake LED flames, or even images of candles you particularly like.

Crystals and Stones

Crystals, gems and even pebbles are all imbued with magic energy. They are as animated as the deer that leaps through the forest or the dolphin in the sea. So treat them with care and respect, and they will care for and respect you back.

I work with crystals a lot. Every time I hold one in my hand, I find it has an electromagnetic energy that sings the word 'magic' to me; I feel its rhythm, its vibration, its connection to me – and me to it and the universe.

Some crystals are aligned more to love (rose quartz) or success (tiger's eye), others to finance or career (malachite). So opt for as good a selection as you can.

Before you use any crystals in your magic work, it's worth letting them know that you are their friend. Cleanse them in spring water and set them out on a window ledge for twenty-four hours to be energised by the sun and moon, and to kick-start their powers. Afterwards, keep your crystals either in a dedicated open box or large organza pouch (they like the light – after all, they've been stuck in the depths of the Earth for thousands of years, so let them reawaken!).

To form a good bond with each stone, perform the relevant ritual (see below). Remember to always find a calm place (your sanctuary, for example), light a candle for atmosphere if required and be centred and find stillness before you begin.

The following is a basic selection of the easiest-to-find crystals to add to your toolbox for manifesting spells. If you can't get hold of one, you can improvise by using one of a similar colour or a favourite pebble as a stand-in, as long as you tell it its intended purpose. (I may use some crystals in the spells section that are not listed below, but the ones here are the most common.)

Citrine

Citrine is a transparent, yellow variety of quartz, ranging from pale to golden yellow to smoky brown, often with rainbow-like occlusions. The name comes from the old French word *citrin*, meaning lemon. Often confused with yellow topaz, citrine was crafted by the Babylonians and ancient Greeks for jewellery and intaglio work.

Citrine is the best stone to use for abundance spells, attracting wealth and prosperity, success and all things that might enrich your life on a material level. Yet it's not a selfish, hoarding stone – it encourages generosity and the possibility for others to share in your good fortune. Sometimes called the 'success stone', it is said to promote good luck in all you do.

Ritual to connect to citrine

After cleansing, hold the stone close to your forehead between your eyebrows – the spot associated with the third-eye chakra (see Glossary, p. 283) and intuitive powers. Close your eyes and affirm to yourself and the stone: 'Thank you citrine for your powers of reward and success in all I do. My gift is to care and keep you safe.'

Keep the citrine under your pillow for one night, and you will have created a strong bond with it, encouraging abundance in your life.

Aquamarine

Known as mermaid's treasure by the ancient Greeks. The word aquamarine comes from the Latin, '*aqua marinus*', meaning 'water of the sea' and referring to its beautiful luminous green/blue colour. Ancient seafarers carried aquamarine with them as a talisman, for good luck and protection, while mediaeval sorcerers used it as a scrying stone by gazing into the crystal to read the future. This was usually performed during a waxing moon, when the stone seemed to align to the lunar phase and turned a more vivid blue.

Wearing aquamarine gives you a dynamic sense of purpose and life direction if you are struggling to know your true pathway. Aquamarine enables you to manifest joy and be empowered with great thoughts and gives you the confidence to follow your dreams. The stone also helps you to take opportunities you have been waiting for.

Ritual to connect to aquamarine

Place the aquamarine in a bowl of spring water and light a blue tea light near by. Gaze into the stone's depths and be aware of the reflections of the dancing candlelight through the water. Be mindful of how this is reflective of your dreams, which rise from the depths of your soul. When you feel ready, take the stone from the water and say: 'Blessed with

19

my dreams, you bless me with your power.' This will deepen your connection.

Malachite

Used as a pigment in green paints from antiquity until as late as 1800. Egyptian pharaohs lined their headwear with malachite to attract the power of the gods. During the medi-aeval period, malachite was carved into amulets and engraved with symbols of the sun, believed to protect the wearer from negative psychic energy.

For manifesting spells, malachite helps you to revise your expectations of what you truly seek (if need be). Well known for its ability to invite both financial and spiritual wealth, it brings richness of mind, body, spirit and soul, and reinforces your magical power to attract what you will. So always make sure you know what you truly want to manifest before you use it!

Ritual to connect to malachite

Take your malachite to a nearby tree of your choice and hold it up against the bark. Close your eyes for a moment to find stillness and be at peace with the tree, then say, 'Thank you for your strength and power to be at my side, for all my posi-tive intentions for wealth, both spiritual and material.' Be mindful of the tree, the malachite and your hand and the natural force flowing through you. You will now be connected to your stone.

Magnetite

Also known in folklore as 'lodestone', meaning 'the stone that leads the way', magnetite is a natural magnet, aligning to the Earth's magnetic field (north and south poles). When you use lodestone, always keep it well away from anything it attracts – i.e. metallic objects (particularly iron) – as it will be less likely to work to your benefit.

Magnetite is a potent stone for manifestation, helping you to draw in what you most long for. This can be anything from desirable outcomes to specific people who can help or mentor you or simply loving attention. It also attracts romantic suitors, commitment and loyalty, and encourages a great rapport with others of your choice.

Ritual to connect to magnetite

Place the stone on a north/south axis with its main point to the north. Sit to the west or east of the stone and form a triangle shape, using the forefingers and thumbs of both hands, over the stone. Find stillness, and then say: 'With this stone my intentions will be safe and will draw what matters to me. Thank you, lodestone, for leading the way for me.'

Clear quartz

Clear quartz is not always as clear as its name suggests. One of the most abundant minerals in the earth, it comes in many forms, sizes and shapes. Most have inclusions (material trapped inside the crystal, such as gas bubbles, radioactive fracture lines and liquids), which are often cloudy and give rise to names such as 'phantom' quartz. Although some witches prefer the translucent or clearest varieties, any inclusions will not affect the properties of the stone.

This stone is often used to amplify intentions in a positive way, connecting you to the highest vibrations of the universe, so it's important you know exactly what you are seeking. When incorporating this crystal into your spell work, what you ask from the universe, you usually get. You can also use clear quartz in tandem with other crystals to amplify their powers.

Ritual to connect to clear quartz

In front of a mirror, light a candle for atmosphere and place the crystal in front of it. Gaze into the flame's reflection in the mirror, then focus on the reflection of the crystal. When you feel calm and centred, say: 'I affirm my connection to the power of this clear quartz and trust its amplifying influence for all my intentions.' Blow out the candle when you feel ready and leave the crystal overnight to charge your home with its empowering energy and connect you to its power.

Tiger's eye

Tiger's eye has shimmering flashes of light due to a mineral deposit within its structure – an iridescent effect known as 'chatoyancy' (deriving from the French name for the more expensive and rarer 'cat's eye' crystal). Tiger's eye and cat's eye were revered in Roman times and feared as 'all-seeing eyes'; they were thought to grant their wearer the ability to see everything, even through closed doors.

Used in spells, tiger's eye enables you to discriminate clearly between what you *think* you need and what you *actually* need. So it is the perfect stone for clarifying whether an intention is truly appropriate for you. As a stone of luck and good fortune, wearing tiger's eye will attract a steady flow of beneficial and successful energy to you.

Ritual to connect to tiger's eye

Place your stone in a sunny window (or outside, somewhere safe, where the sun will shine on it most of the day). Place an oak leaf (or an image of one) beneath the crystal to ground its energy and, when you feel you are ready, say: 'Your eye will see all that needs to be seen, and I thank you for being here with me to help me with my work.' Leave the stone in place until the next day, then use it in spell work to enhance all aspects of good luck.

Turquoise

The name turquoise is derived from the French, *'pierre turqueise'*, meaning 'Turkish stone'. From the second century right through to the sixteenth, trade routes from Asia (where most turquoise was found) crossed through Turkey, which is where early European merchants bought these stones from the local markets. Turquoise has always been considered a protective stone, worn by travellers and traders to promote positive energy.

As a manifestation stone, turquoise can also help to empower you with dynamic and persuasive intentions. Used in spells, the stone attracts career opportunities, lifestyle changes and travel plans.

23

Ritual to connect to turquoise

With your stone in your hand, walk down a quiet footpath, in an easterly direction, and stop when you feel or sense the moment is right for you. (You could even get a sign from the stone to do so – it might warm up in your palm, for example.) Hold the turquoise up to the westward sky to charge it with celestial goodness and to send out your own goodness around the universe. Say, 'Thank you, turquoise for your traveller's joy.' You will now be connected to the stone and its good-luck energy.

Black tourmaline

Once known as 'shorl', black tourmaline has always been considered a stone of protection and is believed to create a psychic shield against negativity. Mediaeval sorcerers would place it in their magic circle to protect against evil spirits.

A powerful grounding stone, it promotes a sense of influence and self-confidence when spell-casting and will help you to achieve success in any long-term project. It also gives you a positive attitude towards your goals and desires and a strong commitment to your intention, so that you physically engage in the process.

Ritual to connect to black tourmaline

Draw a large circle on a piece of paper and place the stone in the centre. Write around the edge of the circle: 'I am protected by this stone, and it will, from now on, help me to achieve my goals.' Leave this in a safe place, until you need to use the stone in your ritual work.

Rose quartz

According to mythology, the crystal was created when Aphrodite's mortal lover, Adonis, was attacked by jealous Ares, who appeared in the form of a boar and gored him to death. As Aphrodite rushed to save him, she caught herself on a thorn, and their mingled blood turned the clear quartz on the ground to pink.

Rose quartz is used in spells both to attract and manifest new love, romance and intimacy, and for its power to create a closer bond between lovers.

Ritual to connect to rose quartz

On the evening of a waxing moon, take a rose (or an image of one), then kiss it to seal your intention for love's magic to work for you. Place the rose quartz beside the rose (or scatter rose petals around the crystal). Leave overnight and, in the morning, keep the crystal on you for one day more, and your connection will be complete.

Amethyst

Many legends surround this beautiful purple quartz stone. Ancient Greeks and Romans routinely studded their drinking goblets with it, believing that wine drunk from the cup would be powerless to intoxicate them, while warriors hung amethyst talismans on their horses' bridles, in the belief that it would make them invincible in battle.

Use this crystal in your spells to reinforce your intentions and to call on the magic of the universe to instil determination and courage to achieve your desire.

Ritual to connect to amethyst

Safely light a blue or purple tea light on the evening of a waning moon. Fill a small bowl with lavender flowers and put your stone in the centre. Consecrate with a few drops of almond oil, and say: 'Amethyst, stay pure for me, to keep me sure that all will be as I desire.' Gaze into the stone for a few minutes and, when you feel centred and ready, blow out the candle. Leave everything in place until the new crescent moon, and your stone will help you to achieve your goals.

Ruby

Although highly prized as a gemstone, and therefore quite expensive to buy, small 'rough rubies' are now easily available and are essential stones for promoting passion, love, success and prosperity. There are numerous myths about this gorgeous red crystal: its ability to instantly boil water when thrown into a cold cooking pot, its power to protect warriors in battle and its red core, lit by the fires of heaven. Ruby has been the stone of rich merchants, kings, queens and emperors, valued for its power to incite love and desire.

Use rough rubies to promote all kinds of passion for people or things, not forgetting to stir desire and encourage success in your spells.

Ritual to connect to ruby

Place your rough ruby in a small bowl and light a red tea light beside it. Watch the flame flicker and burn for a moment or so, then say, 'Thank you, ruby red, for your fire and spirit to always bless my spells with burning passion.' Blow out the candle when you have focused on your crystal for a moment or two, then leave in place for twenty-four hours to charge with positive energy.

Botanicals

All botanicals, whether herbs and other types of plants, trees or shrubs, are instilled with elemental Earth energy (see p. 118) and, like crystals, they are linked to their own specific qualities. For example, lavender is associated with relaxation and protection and sandalwood with harmony and purification; the red rose is symbolic of love and beauty, pink roses, good luck and seduction and white roses, spirituality and peace.

Here is a selection of some of the most popular and widely used botanicals, some of which I have included in spells in this book. Again, you can substitute with others from the Correspondence List (see p. 275) if you can't source the exact ingredient locally.

Flowers, trees, plants

Unless you have a garden or window box, you will either have to purchase flowers and plants or go out into the

countryside and carefully take just a small specimen, without disturbing the plant's reproductive cycle (in other words,
don't dig the whole plant up, and please ask the plant nicely
if it's ok for you to take a leaf or flower before you do so). Also
ensure you are not picking any part of the plant from an
endangered species, or collecting any part of a plant from a
nature reserve, council or privately owned land. However,
cuttings and seeds from small plants can always be grown
indoors or planted out into window boxes.

Fallen leaves, twigs, nuts, fruit and berries, including
acorns, beechnuts, blackberries or sloe berries, obviously,
will be seasonal. But if you fancy performing a spell that
calls on, for example, an acorn, and it is out of season, you
can use an image as a substitute.

Herbs and spices

Herbs can be used in different ways. You can sprinkle them on
to crystals to seal or sanctify the energy of the spell; they can
be made into teas and infusions you might sip during a ritual,
or scattered over incense or candles to reinforce the power of
the spell. The simplest way to store herbs is to dry them (or
buy them already dried) and keep them in a pouch or box. Or
you can grow pots of fresh herbs in your kitchen or on your
windowsill, or, if you have outside space, you can create a herb
garden devoted to those used for cooking and spells.

Basil

Also known as holy basil, this herb is used for love, prosperity and protection manifestation spells. In mediaeval Europe,

basil was thought to attract love, and was often hung in doorways to attract romance, or to ensure that everyone who entered the home was peace-loving. According to traditional British folklore, the scent of fresh basil leaves will calm a lovers' tiff, and gently rubbing a leaf against the skin brings romance into your life.

Mint

According to some accounts, when the Greek god of the underworld, Hades, fell in love with the nymph Minthe, his consort, Persephone, was so jealous that she turned Minthe into the plant. Hades could not transform her back, but he imbued the plant with its mesmerising fragrance, so that the nymph would never be forgotten. With its aromatic leaves and clear scent, mint has the power to enhance desire and promote opportunities to attract wealth.

Sage

Cleansing, protective and healing, sage was used by the ancient Egyptians to boost fertility and by many indigenous peoples to 'smudge' or clear a room or space of negative energy. An old English folk belief held that if sage grew well in the garden, the wife ruled the household! This herb also encourages growth and abundance and ensures that wishes are granted by the universe. Using sage leaves in your spell work also invokes the energy of Zeus (Jupiter) for success and opportunity.

Cinnamon

Readily available as a culinary spice, cinnamon sticks are a better choice than the fine powder, as they can be held or carried for protective power or burned as incense. This is a spice for success, healing, mental clarity, not forgetting attracting money and good luck.

Almond

The almond tree has long been associated with rebirth and vitality. You can buy almonds whole, or you can choose to use almond oil. If you're lucky enough to have an almond tree near you, the twigs and leaves can also be used for money and prosperity spells. Eating almonds is said to feed you with wisdom, and keeping a whole almond in your pocket encourages good luck and abundance.

Apple

The apple was sacred to Aphrodite, and it is still used in many pagan traditions as an ingredient to promote love. If you cut an apple in half widthwise, you'll see that the seeds form the shape of a five-pointed star or pentagram (see p. 112) – a powerful symbol used in all forms of manifesting work. Apple seeds can be added to spells for love, prosperity, fertility, creativity and abundance.

Bergamot

Bergamot is a citrus fruit and is similar to a lemon in shape and texture. It is mostly used as an essential oil, but, if you can get hold of the real thing, keep a leaf in your pocket or wallet to attract success, and to benefit from quick financial gain.

Dandelion

We can all conjure up a vivid image of a dandelion-seed head, and childhood memories of blowing on the seeds to count the hours or days. The dandelion is a useful ingredient in rituals to carry the 'seeds' of our desires to the cosmos.

Lavender

Lavender has been used in love spells for thousands of years for its seductive fragrance and its ability to remove negative intentions. Perhaps best known for its powers to help you sleep and calm and soothe the skin, nerves and mood, it is also thought to promote serenity, grace and elegance in all you do. When used as an essential oil, it removes negativity, and in love it attracts gentleness and purity of spirit.

Olive

The olive was sacred to the Greek goddess Athene and also to the ancient city of Athens, named after her. Wreaths and olive branches were hung over windows and doorways to prevent lightning or block evil spirits from entering the home. Associated with peace, the olive branch is still seen as a symbol of harmony and protection. Olive leaves are used in spells to promote potency, protection, prosperity and success.

Rose

The rose has long been associated with Aphrodite and love. In later Christian iconography, the Virgin Mary was often depicted surrounded by roses. And in the mediaeval allegory the 'Roman de la Rose', a rose garden symbolised both romantic love and Christian perfection. Roses can be used for all kinds of love spells, particularly for manifesting passion, romance and commitment, reinforcing them by using the intoxicating delights of rose essential oils.

Sunflower

This majestic flower turns its head to follow the sun, and its bold, brash, sunny colour, albeit fleeting, reveals its true purpose in spell work to promote self-confidence, vitality, happiness and creativity. Sunflowers may not be easy to find out of season, so substitute with sunflower seeds (any that are left over will be much welcomed by wild birds.)

Oak

In ancient times, the oak was associated with powerful gods all over the world, notably Zeus and Thor. In sacred oak groves, the Great Goddess was believed to share her wisdom through oracular messages, while, according to

Celtic folklore, if you sit under an oak you may hear an oracle whispered to you in the rustling leaves or from a spirit within the trunk. Oak leaves and acorns are often used for protection and strength, fertility, money, success and general good luck.

Beech

Beech is strongly connected to wisdom and ancient learning. It was used to make writing tablets, and, in mediaeval times, thin slices of beech wood were bound together to make the first 'paper' books. Its leaves fall only when new ones have begun to sprout in late autumn, so the beech reminds you to make certain of your future, rather than leave things to chance. You can use beech to help promote your ideas and plans.

Birch

The birch whispers 'trust in your instincts' through its fine leaves – and as the silver birch glistens in the sunlight, it tells you it's time to start afresh. Birch leaves can be used in spells to enhance courage and give you the determination to achieve your dream. This gentle, fragile-looking tree is actually quite hardy and symbolises that in our faults or failings our greatest strength may be found.

Essential Oils

Note: if you have an allergy to essential oils, please don't incorporate them into your practice.

Aromatic oils and essences have been used for thousands of years for medicinal purposes, spiritual healing in perfumery and in witchy potions and brews. The ancient Egyptians used oils for embalming the dead, while the Romans added perfumed oils to their public baths and created scented unguents and powders for their hair, clothes and bodies.

A wide range of essential oils is available these days to enhance and amplify the power of any desired manifestation. Use a drop of oil on a crystal or specific ingredient. This also consecrates or seals your intention to the universe. Essential oils can also be diluted in a carrier oil and dropped on the skin to allure and attract, calm or aid in healing.

The following are the most important oils for manifesting rituals.

Clary sage

Also known as clear-eye, this variety of sage has been used to soothe digestive disorders. In manifestation work, it is used for clarity and for focusing on a clear vision of your future success.

Patchouli

A well-known base note in the perfume industry, the rather dull-looking plant has an enticing, exotic fragrance and evocative name, originating from the Tamil words for 'green' and 'leaf'. It is renowned for relieving stress and for its use in promoting love and desire. In manifesting spells, it is perfect for attracting romance and making a commitment.

Rose and jasmine

Often a little pricy, the good news is that because both are so powerful, you only need the tiniest drop in your spells. These oils are about manifesting love for others, from others and also love of self. If you don't like the sweet, rich musky fragrance of jasmine, then substitute with rose, or vice versa if you find rose too floral.

Ylang ylang

Not only does ylang-ylang oil imbue you with self-confidence, this amazing fragrance is a bit of an aphrodisiac and is renowned for its power to stir passion, increase sexual desire and manifest physical chemistry between two people.

Sandalwood

Known for its anti-inflammatory properties, the wood is often burned as an incense to restore spiritual energy. The oil's soft, woody, earthy fragrance is a powerful addition to manifesting intentions for love relationships, protection and harmony.

Bergamot

The extract from this citrus fruit is well known for its floral yet lemony flavour. Used with care, it is favoured for combatting oily skin and acne, while in manifesting work it is an excellent promoter of success and abundance, and for enhancing self-love.

Oud

An exotic, rare and expensive essential oil, oud comes from the heartwood of the agar tree and is sometimes known as agar-wood oil. Only trees that have been contaminated by a specific fungus (*Phialophora parasitica*) produce this musty, extraordinary fragrance. Used in the perfume industry as a base note, it is a powerful oil for manifesting physical desire, lust, passion and other sensual needs.

Frankincense

Extracted from the boswellia tree, frankincense is known for its spicy, woody, exotic fragrance. Often used for purification incense in sacred places, the oil is said to relieve stress, manifest wealth and success and encourage happiness.

Wild orange

As its name suggests, wild orange is the perfect booster for inspirational living and can promote uplifting thoughts, feelings and the feelgood factor. For manifesting purposes, it encourages creativity, opportunity and adventure and is known as the 'oil of abundance'.

Cedarwood

This warm, woody perfumed oil is renowned for its antibacterial properties and relief from stress and anxiety. When used in spell work, it is uplifting and clears the mind, so you can focus on what you truly want and 'see the wood' for the trees.

RITUAL TO CONSECRATE BOTANICALS AND ESSENTIAL OILS

It's easy to assume that our jars of dried herbs and tiny phials of essential oils seem lacking in life. But, in fact, everything natural is filled with magic and needs to be respected and honoured before being incorporated into your spell work.

This simple ritual will cover all botanicals, oils, candles and other ingredients in your possession. Whenever you add new ones to your collection, simply place them on your altar for one hour and do the following:

With your writing hand, point your finger over the plant/bottle/leaves/flowers and draw in the air over the item/s the sign of a pentagram (see p. 112 for how to do this). Repeat eight more times, and the object/s will be honoured and consecrated with your personal power, in magical alignment with the universe.

Colour

The symbolic use of colour is vital to witchcraft manifestation. Symbols are deeply embedded in our collective unconscious, so most of us instinctively know red is associated with passion and fire, blue with feeling and water, yellow for ideas, intellectual pursuits and so on.

So when we choose a red crystal or a green candle, we are reinforcing certain principles concerning these colours and adding energy associated with their qualities. In Eastern philosophies, seven colours are associated with the seven main chakras (see Glossary, p. 283).

The following is a brief guide to the key meanings of the most popular colours used in modern witchcraft for manifesting. These can be added in spell work in the form of candles, crystals, flowers, ribbon, twine or images. Enhance the colour of your choice by wearing matching jewellery, crystals or clothes.

Red

Associated with the magical element Fire, the planet Mars and the astrological sign of Aries, red is the colour of passion, arousal, willpower and vitality. Used in spells, it invokes action and fiery love relationships, inviting you to take control of your life and engage with your intention for success, rather than sit around twiddling your thumbs.

Blue

Blue is soothing. It invokes serenity and peace, yet it can also instil trust and positive communication if you're looking for good influences in your life. Associated with Jupiter (which originally ruled both Sagittarius and Pisces – the latter is now said to be ruled by Neptune), it is inspiring and yet pacifying; it is the perfect colour to include in your spell palette both to augment positivity and subdue negativity.

Yellow/orange

Associated with Gemini, Mercury and the sun, yellow and light shades of orange brighten our lives, attract others to us and enhance all spells related to manifesting brilliant ideas, business goals, property deals and success. They also enable you to think logically, persuade others and have self-confidence in all you do.

Green

Green is associated with planet Earth, nature, the element Earth and, in traditional folk magic, fertility and forest deities. It is an essential colour for grounding your intention, fertilising and bringing it to fruition and the future 'harvest' of your goal. Darker shades of green, such as in the crystal malachite, are used in business and financial spells, invoking prosperity and spiritual wealth in the form of self-realisation.

White

Associated with purity, peace and spiritual grace, this 'colour' is, of course, about the absence of colour – yet also like a prism, it is all colour, too. Clear quartz, opals and moonstones fall into the 'white' category and can be reinforced with a white candle or ribbon to promote sincerity, purity and sacred illumination when working your manifesting spells.

Black

Linked with Saturn, Capricorn and sometimes Scorpio, black, like white, is a non-colour. Yet it is thought to be one of the most potent symbols of protection, self-empowerment and counter-negativity. Stabilising and yet provocative, black can help to draw wealth (all kinds) to you and, simultaneously, protect you from those who might cast negative psychic thoughts or energy upon you.

Violet/purple

Because of an association with the third-eye chakra, various shades of purple (such as that of amethyst) have long been connected to spirituality, psychic awareness and intuition. Darker shades of violet are linked with positions of power and can be included in your spells for career or worldly ambition. Light violet and lavender enhance the purity of your intention, but also promote a deep desire for the good of all.

Pink

A magical colour associated with Venus, Taurus and Libra, pink is important for attracting new romance, committing yourself to a long-term love affair or for success in any kind of relationship. Adding pink crystals (such as rose quartz and rhodochrosite) will attract harmony and affection – the perfect colour for manifesting successful partnerships.

Now that you have all the basic ingredients for casting spells (and you can, of course, add more to reinforce your intentions or to act as substitutes, as suggested in the Correspondence List on p. 275), it's time to open yourself up to manifesting spells.

CHAPTER THREE

Let's Get Practical

'Tis now the very witching time of night . . .
**William Shakespeare, English
playwright, poet and actor**

In this chapter, you will find the various techniques used in witch manifestation spells, as well as learn how to create your sacred space and how to protect your spells – and yourself – from negativity.

Visualisation

I often use visualisation rituals in this book. Visualisation is simply using the power of your imagination (the intuitive, right side of your brain), along with all your senses to 'see' a goal or intention. This then leads on to actualising it. The imagination (according to esoteric tradition) is a direct pathway to the sacred soul of oneself and its connection to the universe. Visualisation is more than just a snapshot in your mind, though – it's more like a full-on video.

Let's take visualising a cup of tea as an example:

* Imagine you are putting some tea in a pot. (What colour is the pot? What type of tea are you using?)

* Next, imagine you are boiling the kettle. (Visualise how much water you put in. Is it an electric kettle?)

* Now, imagine pouring the water into the pot and letting the tea steep.

* Imagine the cup, the saucer – what do they look like?

* What is the first taste like? Is the tea too hot? Too strong? Too weak?

The more detail you add to your 'video' scene (and it doesn't have to be a cup of tea – it can be coffee or your drink of choice), the more you engage in the process of it happening. And the more real it feels to you, the more real it will become in your life.

Similarly, if you are hoping to manifest an ambition, provide your brain with as many details about your goal as possible. The more you include in your visualisation, the more likely that you will achieve the desired outcome.

Try this visualisation exercise:

1. Find a quiet place where you won't be disturbed. You can sit or stand – it's up to you.

2. Still your mind by breathing slowly in and out through your nose.

3. Close your eyes (or you can leave them open, but to begin with it's easier to have them closed, so you don't get distracted).

4. Hold a crystal of your choice to your navel.

5. When you are feeling calm and relaxed, start off by thinking about a simple intention you have today – one that you are almost certain will happen (such as meeting that friend for lunch, going to the hairdresser, getting the hoovering done, running a bath).

6. Put your thoughts into 'video mode' in your imagination. The more you can visualise this simple intention in your mind, the more you will be getting in touch with your deepest self.

7. After a few minutes of visualising the 'event' and what happens, come back to your normal mode and return to doing ordinary things, letting the energy disperse into the universe.

Later on, when the 'intention' plays out in real life, notice what actually takes place. How close was your visualisation to reality?

Remember: your imagination is the pathway to your inner witch – so use it!

Journal Writing

Writing your intentions down is a positive way to reveal your desires to the universe, plus it can help you to keep check of the stages in the process.

In your journal, set out the original intention (with pictures or cut-out images, if you prefer), then make notes about anything significant that happens, perhaps using the lunar phases (new crescent moon, waxing moon, full moon, waning moon – more on these on p. 91) as dates to make note of your progress along the way. Observing how your intention is playing out in this way will help you to realise how your actual engagement with it brings it to life.

Write verses, poems or flashes of insight, jot down any lyrics or songs that come to mind, and reflect on what it all might mean in relation to your intention. Any kind of writing, note-making or artwork keeps up a steady flow of creativity between you and the universe, and is a powerful way to channel your desire. The amount that you personally invest in this intention is also key to achieving it.

Another way to use your journal is to write down meaningful signs from the universe. For example, you might write: 'It was a new moon and I saw a stranger in town – what does this mean to me?' Finding meaningful coincidences (or 'synchronicity', as analytical psychologist Carl G. Jung called it) is one of the most inspiring and thought-provoking ways to express your manifestation process. Once you start noticing signs and signals from the universe, you begin to realise which ones are telling you that you are on the right track. It's almost as if something out there is beckoning to you – urging you to carry on, to keep believing, keep looking, keep acting. This creates a new awareness that your message in a bottle has arrived at the place it's meant to be in the universe.

So look out for these moments. Scribble them in your journal – because if they mean something to you, they are signposts to your success.

BOOK OF SHADOWS

Wiccans who practise witchcraft usually keep a book (rather like a mediaeval grimoire) containing details of spells and rituals, ingredients and secret incantations. Back in the 1940s, Gerald Gardner (see p. 9) proposed that covens should keep such a work exclusively for their own use, and he dubbed it the 'Book of Shadows'. Since the 1970s, these have been used by all kinds of witches. You could keep a journal filled with notes, observations, spells, herbal and other folklore and rituals and call it your Book of Shadows (or any other title of your choosing) to give it an aura of mystery and magic.

Manifestation – What Is It?

The word 'manifest' comes from the Latin word *manifestus*, meaning clear, apparent or evident. In other words, manifesting is about making something happen in your personal reality – perhaps a dream of financial stability, a country lifestyle or a happy family. You can make these dreams come true (or bring them into tangible reality) only if you are truly honest about what you seek. Once you start to really believe in yourself – and by believe, I mean know or experience your true self – you can then manifest that which you desire.

47

In fact, manifestation is the main goal of the witch's practice, forming the basis of all conjuring, summoning, engaging, intuiting and magic. So if you learn to harness the power of your inner witch, you can amplify and promote your ability to make your dreams come true.

Manifestation Wish List

Most of us have dreams and desires we would like to manifest, whether long- or short-term. Throughout history and around the world, superstitions, charms, talismans and spells have been cast to make those dreams come true. Many people still wish on stars, throw coins in a fountain or 'scatter money on the floor, and watch it come in through the door'. There is even an old sailor's belief that if you make a wish when you see flying fish leaping across the bow waves, you will be given whatever you wish for at your next port of call.

Witches' Secret Words

A witch's mantra, whether a single line or more, can be an instant connection to your inner witch. Rhyming verse amplifies the power of the rhythms of language, which is why spells are often written this way, as seen in one version of the 'Witches' Rede':

To bind the spell every time,
let the spell be spake in rhyme.

Rhythm and rhyme create an empowering force, not only in the mind, but also in the universe, and that's to do with music.

This kind of rhyming flow comes easily to some, whereas others may struggle with it. So I'm not going to tell you to write rhymes or poetry (unless you want to). But the most powerful spells are often the ones you create yourself. They can be a flowing stream of consciousness, illogical and meaningless to anyone else, but as long as they mean something to you that's all that matters. Spells and incantations written by you will empower *you* – because they speak from the heart.

For a magical incantation or mantra, you can just use one line or a simple word (like 'abracadabra'), phrase, rhyme or quote that you love. Your personal mantra will help you to switch instantly from logical left-brain thinking to your intuitive, soulful, witchy self.

Repeat your mantra whenever you feel like it; or perhaps write it at the front of your journal or on a Post-it note stuck to your fridge door or make-up mirror. It will always remind you that within you is the witch. Then perhaps tag on to the end of your mantra this reminder: 'I connect now with the mystery of nature and the universe, which is the witch in me.'

Creating a Sanctuary or Altar

Now that you have your mantra, you'll need to create a sanctuary or special place in which to perform your work.

Your sacred space is a private store for your witchcraft ingredients; a place to gather and take pride in your

49

collection of crystals, candles, ribbons, images, journal, spell book and so on. When you first initiate yourself into the hidden powers within you, and access your inner witch, this special place will help you to feel secure and empowered in your own private world.

Choose a space where you won't be disturbed by anyone or anything (and that includes mobile phones – leave all your devices in another room). It may seem obvious, but any intrusions, noise or text messages will simply cut through the deeper connections you are making, and you'll lose touch with your magic synergy.

Set up your altar, table or whatever you prefer to call your sacred space. Decorate it with anything that creates the right kind of atmosphere for you personally – images, a mirror, candlesticks, jars of herbs, essential oils, a pile of ancient grimoires or witch spell books, for example. A few green plants might work, too, for good energy, a box of crystals for your manifesting spells and also a large clear quartz crystal to amplify and energise all your spell work. You could also lay out a grid of smaller crystals to promote positivity and success (see p. 54).

Even if your space is just the corner of a table or a section of floor, it is your sacred altar, so treat it as such. Never let anyone else use it, or you will be left with their psychic dust (spiritual energy – friendly or otherwise) everywhere.

Accessories

You may like to decorate your space with some traditional witch's paraphernalia – such as a wand (made from a fallen branch or twigs of willow, ash, apple or oak, bound with coloured ribbons representing symbolic energies), which can be used to direct energy during spells or to cast a magic circle (see p. 120). A chalice, cup or cauldron can also be included as 'props' or for atmosphere.

Alternatively, you might prefer to hang symbols on your wall, if you have space – perhaps a large pentagram (see p. 112), a poster of the lunar cycles, a list of sabbats, images of your preferred deities or animal totems, if used. You could write out the complete 'Witches' Rede' and pin it to your wall, reminding you of what Wicca is all about, too.

If you are currently working towards one achievable goal (or more), you could make up a mood board, pinning up or sticking on images that relate to this. Your goal may be as abstract (in the sense that it's an emotional one) or as real as you like, as long as it is feasible.

Here are some other smaller items you could include in your sanctuary:

* Tea lights (you can light these for atmosphere whenever you sit down to write, for example)

* A pile of parchment-style or heavy watercolour paper for writing out spells

* Pen and ink (it's always nice to write with a fountain pen and scrawl across a piece of parchment-style paper)

* A collection of divinatory tools, such as tarot cards, runes, a scrying mirror (scrying is the practice of gazing into a mirror or other reflective surface and divining the future from the shapes or patterns seen)

51

* Assorted symbolic objects, such as keys, totems, photos of ancestors and so on

Your journal or Book of Shadows could take pride of place. And finally, if you have a long-term goal or dream, find an image of what that means to you, and place it on your altar/table or your wall.

Blessing your space

Once you have designated your sacred space and got the main elements in place, it's time to cleanse all negative energy from it.

Light a sage smudge stick (you can buy these online, but avoid white sage, as this is now a rare herb – any other form of sage will do) and walk around the room, waving the smoking stick in every corner, under every chair and beneath your altar or table, too, repeating aloud: 'I am cleansing this space of all negativity.' All psychic and geopathic stress (see Glossary, p. 283) will be cleared away, too.

Once you feel you have smudged everywhere, thank the sage for clearing the space for you and blow out your stick.

Element blessing

Next, ask the blessing of the elements and the four directions (see p. 141) to protect your space.

Light a small white tea light and repeat the following incantation at each compass direction, as you turn in an anti-clockwise direction:

East and Air, bless this space so I may see.
West and water, bless this place with love for me.
North and Earth, make real and true my goals.
South and Fire, then let my heart unfold.

Now take a moment to feel centred and find stillness, before saying, 'With this candle flame, I make this space my own, free from all negativity and blessed by the light of the universe.'

Blow out the candle and your sanctuary will now be ready for you to do your great work.

Protection Ritual

You've got your sacred space set up, cleansed and blessed, so all that's left for you to do is to ensure that you are personally protected.

But think about this: whether you use rituals, spells, incantations or divination tools, call on spirits, the divine or just your friendly crystal, you are creating a sort of 'butterfly effect' across the universe. (Based on the work of American meteorologist Edward Lorenz, this is the idea that small, seemingly insignificant events can lead to something much bigger – in this case a butterfly flapping its wings may result in a tornado further down the line.) So when you're blasting off your intentions into the universe, you and your goal need to be protected from any other kind of negative 'butterfly effect' that may be going around.

To be in complete harmony with the universal forces with which you are working, this protection grid will ensure that you are guarded from any negative psychic or geopathic stress (see Glossary, p. 283) that might be emanating from invisible forces when you practise.

The grid

This crystal grid can be left in your sacred place or altar to keep it pure, sanctified, protected and safe. Lay the grid out on the evening of a waxing moon to energise and maximise its power.

You will need:

* 5 pieces of black tourmaline (for protection)
* 5 pieces of clear quartz crystal (for reinforcement)

1. Choose a place where the grid won't be disturbed (except when you decide to give the place a clean).
2. Start with one black tourmaline to the north, one to the south, one to the west and one to the east. Place the fifth in the centre.
3. Place four clear quartz crystals between each of the black stones to create a circle of black, clear, black, clear and so on.
4. Hold the last piece of clear quartz in your hand and say:
   This stone so clear it fills my air,
   Lies side by side with stones so fair.
   Protected now my shrine will be
   And none will cast dark thoughts on me.
5. Place the last piece of quartz to the south of the bottom black stone.

Leave the whole set-up in place as your permanent protection grid.

Intention Practice

A good way to practise intention setting before you get to do it for a long-term goal is by setting one simple intention daily. At the beginning of each day, say aloud to yourself – and to the universe – what you intend to happen that day. First, say each of these phrases, then follow with your actual goal:

* 'Today I do my best to achieve this goal.'

* 'I look for the positive side of everything.'

* 'I am a child of the universe, and it is my right to be happy.'

* 'I am true to my authentic self.'

Next, say, 'My intentional goal today is . . .' and recite nine times (nine being a mystical number). To help you set your intention in stone (literally), take a piece of clear quartz and hold it in your hand as you repeat it. Clear quartz amplifies your intentions and sends them flying high with goodness to the universe. This not only helps you to realise that you will have to act on your intention, but also aligns you with the energy of the world around you.

You may for example, say, 'My intentional goal today is to devote more time to my creative talent.' Well, if you know what that is, and what needs to be done, then do it. Because unless you actually engage in that intention (for example, get out the paintbrush if you're an artist), it isn't going to happen.

Be humble, gracious, grateful and, most of all, realistic with this process. Don't be led astray by impossible dreams.

Once you have achieved a few 'simple intentions' over a series of days, you can start to work towards a more life-changing one.

Favourable Times for Manifesting Spells

It helps to know the most auspicious times to put your thoughts into practice, so below is a brief guide to when you should work your magic for intention setting and getting. As you read on through this book, you will find more detailed information about seasons, sabbats, timings and lunar cycles, so you can really focus on performing practices at the right time and with the right energy for manifesting your goals. Finally, with your chosen timing, always cast intentions for things you know you truly seek – not what other people think you want or what they want.

The following are some of the most favourable times to 'fire' your intentions and practise manifestation – times when the magic of the universe can help you to achieve your goals:

* According to the energy of the lunar cycle (see pp. 91–4)

* On days such as equinoxes and solstices and other witch's sabbats (see p. 130)

* Your birthday

* If you gaze at the stars at night and see a falling star

* A day when you simply feel at one with the universe or just feel good to be you

* When you get a 'sign' from the universe – maybe a butterfly lands on your shoulder, a bird sings when you least expect it, you experience a moment of fascinating synchronicity . . . whatever 'feels' or seems special or meaningful

* When you find a stone, plant or fallen leaf that seems to 'smile' positive energy at you

* Moments when you can really relax, meditate and switch off from the material world

Be a Proactive Witch

We all deserve to have what we want in life, but only if it is truly an expression of our authentic selves. So if you can raise your eyes to the sky, put your hands in prayer pose, close your eyes and trust in the universe, and truly believe in your goal, it will oblige.

Graciousness and gratitude go hand in hand. Say, 'Thank you, universe, for understanding that this is what I have asked for. It is already mine – I only have to wait for it to appear in my life.'

57

This doesn't mean you can sit around waiting for something to just drop out of the sky, though. It might, with luck. But the law of probability is just as relevant here as the law of attraction, so to really give life to your intention you need to engage with it, too.

The art of witchcraft manifestation is about following up your work. For example, when you're hoping for a new job, you need to go out and actively look for one. If you're looking for a new lover, you have to put yourself out there and so on. So don't be a lazy witch. Action and engagement with your goal will give you a better chance of success than letting the unforgiving element of 'chance' take over.

Letting Go

Once you have fired your intention into the universe with the help of your spell work, you have to let go of it and trust in the process.

If you've ever written a book or painted a work of art, you'll know how hard it can be to down tools. Creative work involves titivating, adding, editing, cutting, changing a word here or a colour there – but there's usually a moment when, intuitively, you know when to stop. Similarly, with sending off your intention, you have to 'stop' the spell at some point. You'll know when the moment is right, and, once you have had a little practice in 'letting go', it gets more intuitive.

When you have finished your spell, thank yourself for stopping when and where you have, and remind yourself of how important that is. This is often the hardest part for a lot of people because they think if they don't keep doing the same practice over and over again, it won't work. Manifestation is knowing that something is happening from the moment you let go. You can keep repeating in your mind what your intention is but, once the ritual is performed, don't think that if you do it again, it will make it work more quickly. It is not important how long the 'happening' takes – you need only smile and engage with the universe, knowing that what you seek is already yours.

To help with this, say frequently to yourself, 'I have the most power when I let go of that power, and know what I desire is already mine'.

You should now be familiar with the principles and practices that can be used to manifest your goals. Read on to discover how to access your inner witch.

CHAPTER FOUR

Access Your Inner Witch

Hope is the thing with feathers that perches in the soul – and sings the tunes without the words – and never stops at all.
Emily Dickinson, 1830–1866
(American poet)

So now you understand the mechanics of manifestation, witchcraft and of your conscious intentions, you need to get to know that inner, less well-known you, and how to connect to your witchy self.

But first, a few more of the basics . . .

The Witch's Code

Before you begin any manifesting work, you need to ensure not only that it is goodness for yourself that you are seeking, but that you won't hurt anyone else in the process. This means honouring what is known as 'the witch's code'. It is an informal ethical code, and anyone who practises any form of witchcraft is wise to follow it because, as they say, what goes around, comes around, and, if you're not sending out utter and true belief in the process and in yourself, deceit and untruth will find their way back to you.

Here is my summary of the three main tenets of the code:

1. **The power of three** As mentioned, what you put out into the world will come back to you, and usually three times more powerfully, according to witchcraft belief. So the spells or practices you perform to manifest results are not just about creating goodness for yourself, but for everyone and everything on this planet (and beyond.) Just be careful not to fall into the trap of casting spells to try to persuade or control other people's desires, or they will start controlling yours, too. Control attracts control.

2. **The Wiccan Rede** The rede, meaning advice, is a state-ment often included in the witch's code. There is a twenty-four-line poem (also known as 'The Wiccan Rede', thought to have been written at some point during the twentieth century), but a shorter rhyming couplet (believed to be taken from the longer version; or possibly the longer one was written around the couplet!) was popularised by the English Wiccan Doreen Valiente in the 1960s. The simplest of many versions of one particular line is: 'An it harm none, do what ye will.' In other words: 'Do what you like, as long as you don't harm anything in the world, including yourself.'

3. **You get what you wish for** They say you should be care-ful what you wish for, and this is very true. For example, you may wish you could travel the world like your pal who

seems to be having a wonderful time and has created vast social media hype around their trip. Then you get what seems to be a lucky break and are able to do the same trip yourself. Your wish has come true, but with it come new responsibilities and demands you hadn't anticipated, which, in turn, create a wave of unwanted knock-on effects.

Each time you seek out or have an 'intention' to manifest, remember to focus for a moment on the modern witch's code. It's worth writing down the points above on a piece of paper and placing it in your sanctuary (see p. 49) or another designated spot, where you will see it daily as a reminder.

The Witch's Manifesto

Below is what I call the witch's manifesto, and it is all about remembering various points to help you focus on your intention. Again, you might want to write these points down somewhere – perhaps in your journal or on a piece of card or paper in a conspicuous place (perhaps your altar – see p. 49) – and refer to them as often as you can.

* **Intention** Be absolutely clear in your mind and in your heart what you intend to manifest or achieve. Write it down. Question your motives.

* **Confidence** Affirm to yourself that you have the will and determination to succeed. Write this down. (Practise the 'Ritual to Encourage Self-confidence' on p. 77 whenever you feel confidence is lacking.)

* **Courage** Be aware that some spells require not only integrity and self-belief, but often a hefty dose of courage, too. Armed with the kind of courage that says, 'I'm not afraid to believe in my dream coming true' or, 'I'm not afraid to take a leap in the dark,' who dares usually wins.

* **Secret** Once you have fired your desire and cast your spell, never reveal to *anyone* what you have asked for, what you have done or why. Intrusive psychic energy from other people can create havoc with the pure power of the spell.

* **Manifest** Remember that your desire to manifest will only work once you have dedicated yourself to the intention and are actively engaged in the creative process of your goal. For example, you might cast a spell to encourage romance into your life, but you will still need to make the effort to go out and meet new people – romance isn't going to fall out of the sky and into your lap.

Next up are some exercises to discover the deeper hidden powers within you.

....

THE WITCHING HOUR RITUAL

On the day of a waxing or full moon, stand outside, alone, where there is no one in sight, maybe with a view of the hills, countryside, the sea – anywhere peaceful and surrounded by nature, where you can see trees, breathe fresh air, see clouds or blue sky, and are not hemmed in by high buildings, power lines, busy shopping centres, polluted pavements and cars. Nature breathes her own magic, and it is this energy you need to breathe in.

1. Once you are standing still in your chosen spot, raise your arms to the sky, then draw them down to give yourself a big hug, as if gathering in all the sky above you, hugging that to you, too.

2. Close your eyes and imagine the sun filling every cell in your body with light. In fact, you are so illuminated that you can see deep within you, not the visceral you – the blood, the guts, the brain cells – but another inner you, illuminated by the sun's rays, like a beacon of light within your soul self.

3. As you scan eternity within, you see another light in the distance. The light begins to glow brighter, as if someone is coming towards you with a torch.

3. Your own solar glow flashes into their light, and your lights meet in the darkness. As you get closer, you see yourself; this is no reflection, but your inner witch who has come to meet you and welcome you to join her in the cosmic dance.

4. Say 'Yes,' and smile at your inner witch, acknowledging her presence by raising and opening your arms to the sky, releasing your inner witch back into the universe where magic happens. Her light disappears, but you know she is always there, within and without you.

5. Come out of your visualisation slowly, open your eyes and walk a little to bring yourself back to a normal mindset.

After this ritual you may feel different (as if you've discovered a treasure within you), and you may not. If nothing happened, try it again. If you're sceptical, wonder why you are sceptical.

This is the thing: if nothing happens, that's because you don't believe in things happening enough. But once you fill yourself with self-belief and belief in the happening (repeat the rituals on pp. 79 and 86 if necessary), then 'trying' to access your inner witch won't be necessary – because you'll know she is always there.

....

RITUAL FOR BEING IN HARMONY WITH THE WORLD AROUND YOU

Use this ritual to connect your inner witch, the outer you and nature in a harmonious way.

You don't have to go out in the countryside for this one, but it helps to do so, as it will immerse you in the elemental energies of Fire, Air, Earth and Water (see p. 115)

1. Go for a walk.

2. Be mindful of the walking: be aware that as you walk, each step you take connects you to the ground (Earth); each breath you take connects you to the Air; every landscape brings you in harmony with the bigger picture (Fire); and every feeling you feel is bringing you closer to your feelings and intuition (Water).

2. Walk as far as you like and sing, hum or whistle a tune to uplift and inspire you and connect you to nature. Once you feel enlivened, it's time to carry this harmonious energy back home with you.

4. Stop when you see a friendly stone and say hello to it. For a moment, let it speak to you if you like, opening your mind to what it might say, and how it wants to be your friend. Gently place it in your palm, give it a warm squeeze of friendship, then, as long as you have permission to do so, put it in a bag or pocket and take it home.

Carefully put your stone on a surface where you can see it every day to remind you of how you are now in tune with nature.

Develop Your Intuition

Intuition is a very personal thing. You may experience it as a moment of grand awakening, an epiphany or an intuitive 'knowing' – a deep universal truth. It can appear as a fleeting moment when you 'spot' the parking space around the next corner; you might think of someone, and then five minutes later they call you; or you might make a decision, based not on logic or calculation but on a deep feeling – you may call it gut instinct.

Intuition originates from the right side of the brain, where it combines with deeper, unknown forces and your imagination to work mysteriously together. Developing your intuitive power will help you to access the voice of your inner witch, who 'knows' deep down what is true and, ultimately, what the universe is saying.

VISUALISATION FOR TRUSTING
YOUR INTUITION

Can you imagine this inner place we call 'intuition'? As an abstract concept, it's not easy to grasp, so let's imagine it to be a 'thing'.

1. Close your eyes and place both forefingers on the bridge of your nose, perhaps the fingers overlapping, to make a downward V shape over your eyes with your hands, thumbs resting on chin.

2. Sit like this for a few minutes and visualise a golden ball of light that sleeps deep within you, behind your eyes.

3. Become aware of your breath, gently and deeply moving in and out.

4. Now imagine the golden ball awakening, vibrating in rhythm with your breathing. Press gently with your fingers.

5. Open your eyes and imagine or 'see' that the ball has appeared before you. It is now 'out there', and it speaks to you: 'I am the golden ball of intuition. If you listen to my voice, you will know the truth.'

6. Close your eyes again and let the ball return to sleep in your mind.

You can call on and trust in this golden ball of intuition to replace and override overt logic, overthinking or a more calculated mindset by pressing your forefinger to this place on your forehead at any time.

Intuition in practice

Next time you are out and about, just suddenly stop for a moment – at any moment that you 'sense' is right. Stop and sit (or stand, if you prefer) and just stop whatever you were doing.

Take a few deep, calm breaths to find stillness, and listen to the sounds around you. It may be traffic, birds tweeting, music in a shopping mall. Whatever it is, just listen. Place one forefinger on the bridge of your nose and press gently to connect with and awaken your intuitive mind (the golden ball). It is at this exact place that you intuitively knew when to stop, and it is here again where you will intuitively know when to start walking again. Can you hear the 'voice' of the golden ball within? Can you feel the moment appearing to you? See yourself about to walk again? Feel it in your gut – that it's time to act, NOW?

This is your intuition working on a very simple level, but that moment you choose to stop and the moment you choose to start again are intuitive ones. Trust in these kinds of moments. Why not practise visualising the parking space before you get there? Or the friend you're about to bump into in the street? Or the phone call you were expecting?

Open up to your 'right-side brain', where your intuition and imagination lead you to your psychic sense and beyond, and there you will discover your inner witch hidden in the magical realm of your soul.

Having discovered your inner witch, the power of manifesting and the more practical aspects of witchcraft, you are ready to begin your quest in the next chapter.

CHAPTER FIVE

Witch Wisdom

It had long since come to my attention that people of accomplishment rarely sat back and let things happen to them. They went out and happened to things.
Leonardo da Vinci, Italian painter, engineer, scientist, humanist

In this chapter, you will learn how to harness confidence and self-belief, establish your needs and desires and, most importantly, your true values and what matters most to you. A little self-awareness will serve you well and encourage you to be true to your authentic desires as you work with the power of manifesting and witchcraft.

Be Aware of Who You Are

Before you leap into trying out any spell to manifest your desires, self-esteem, self-confidence, self-belief and self-awareness are fundamental. You have to anchor true belief and confidence in yourself and acknowledge and accept your feelings, both good and not so good (see below). In fact, once you have mastered these, so as to cultivate self-understanding, the universe will find it easier to understand you, too.

By drawing on the magic of your inner witch, and finding your own power, you will be free to manifest goodness in your life. Everything you dream of can be yours, with a little help from your inner witch, once you know what you truly seek and what is good for you.

Value your feelings

Of course, everyone doubts themselves at some point. We all worry we aren't 'good enough', especially when we follow other people in the media, social or otherwise. But this comparison thing is very unkind, and it makes some of us feel low on self-confidence, unloved or unworthy: do I deserve to be a witch? Do I deserve to be loved? Do I deserve to get what I desire?

Well, yes, you do, just by virtue of being a human being on this planet. You have a right to feel things, and to be emotionally invested in life, filled with love, desire, anger and hate. These are all ordinary human feelings.

But never doubt your gut instinct or intuition – because these are the most important devices in your witch's toolbox.

Now let's get practical. Try out the simple exercise that follows to help dump self-doubt if you have any. Self-doubt sabotages your values and undermines your confidence and sense of power, and it's the first thing you need to address before you start practising.

RITUAL TO BANISH SELF-DOUBT

Sitting quietly in a calm place, or outside under the stars (wherever feels peaceful and where you won't be interrupted), perform the following during each waning-moon phase (after a full moon and before a new moon) as part of your practice. If you repeat it regularly, you will be more able to trust your intuition and your instincts, and free yourself from dependence on what society, peers, family members or others think.

1. Close your eyes, place your thumbs under your chin with your hands framing your face and say, 'I am holding my head high with desires, dreams and goals.'

2. Next, cross your arms, place your hands on your shoulders and say, 'I am solid and grounded. I need only connect to the universe to release all negativity.'

3. Place your hands over your navel, left hand over right, and say, 'Here is the centre of my being. I am centred and I trust in myself.'

4. Cross your arms again and place your hands on opposite knees. Say, 'I have no weakness. I will not bend at the knee to fall down, only to prove my adaptability, my respect and happiness for joining in the music of the universe.'

5. Finally bend over, trying to keep your legs straight, your head resting on your knees, perhaps, and a hand under each foot. (If this is too difficult, just bend over as far as you can, letting your arms hang

down, and imagine your hands touching the ground.) Say, 'I have no fear of self. I have no doubt of self or of my intentions. I am myself and I am part of the cosmos with my feet placed upon this earth.'

6. When you feel ready, release your hands, slowly roll up, vertebra by vertebra, to standing and open your eyes.

Look at the world around you with a revised perspective. You will feel value in yourself and your role in the cosmos. If you don't immediately feel this way, repeat this ritual as frequently as you like, until you do.

Self-esteem

Before you can build or nurture self-confidence, you need a healthy sense of self-esteem. This, in turn, encourages confidence to grow. Self-esteem is about feeling good about yourself, knowing your true values and what is important to you. It is also about asserting yourself, nurturing your strengths and accepting your weaknesses.

With a little more awareness of what truly matters to you in life, and therefore what your values are, you will gain more self-esteem. And with self-esteem, you can open doors and seize opportunities that you may have avoided or not even thought possible before.

RITUAL TO ENCOURAGE
POSITIVE SELF-ESTEEM

Choose a tree that you find majestic, empowering, beautiful or mysterious, or one that you just admire. You may not happen upon it straight away – it may take you an afternoon's walk in the country, or it may take just a minute, as you spot a bending willow or a towering oak in the park – but finding your own special tree that 'speaks' to you will begin to enrich you with a sense of what you value.

1. Either at sunrise, or as early as you can in the morning, stand before your tree.

2. Touch its bark.

3. Close your eyes for a few seconds and reflect on why you feel an affinity with this tree. Ask yourself: 'why do I find this tree beautiful or admirable; what is it I identify with?' Does it inspire you? Does it motivate you? Does it energise you? Think about the following:
   - What other things or people make you feel like this?
   - What have this tree and all these things that give you a sense of excitement, wonder or joy got in common?

4. Imagine spreading your mind outwards like the branches of the tree.

5. Imagine you are gathering in the 'air of self-esteem' into your being. Like a tree, you are taking in nutrients (in this case 'esteem'), and, in return, you are giving out the value of yourself to the world.

6. Breathe this sense of 'value' in and out slowly. Feel it growing as strong as the tree.

7. As you breathe in and out, imagine your true self-esteem growing like the tree, getting stronger every day.

8. Hold the image of the tree as a nurturing force inside you for a few more minutes, always keeping you worthy and filled with self-esteem and self-love.

Whenever you feel a lack of self-esteem, either visit your tree or just visualise it inside you, as you slowly breathe its nurturing power in and out. Practise this ritual as many times as you desire to imbue yourself with the natural tenacity to manifest your goals.

Self-confidence

What is self-confidence? Self-confidence doesn't grow on trees, but it does grow alongside the large helpings of self-esteem you have now discovered by 'branching out'.

Some people appear so confident and sure of themselves. They display arrogance, boast about their achievements and can't wait to tell others what they know. This overt display of pride usually comes before the proverbial fall.

Genuine self-confidence isn't about lauding and shouting off about yourself – it's about a quiet inner sense of self-reliance and integrity. It's a confidence that doesn't rely on others to make you feel good to be you, and it's a confidence that says, 'I trust in myself – me – more than anyone else.'

RITUAL TO ENCOURAGE SELF-CONFIDENCE

Here's a magic trick to help your integrity blossom, so that you can get started on your witch work. Perform this regularly, if you need to – perhaps every full moon – to re-ignite that confidence spark within.

You will need:
* 7 basil leaves (for protection and grounding)
* 7 small pieces of clear quartz crystal (for spirit and clarity)

1. On a table or flat surface, lay the basil leaves in a horizontal line and form a cross by placing the crystals in a vertical line through it. Place the fourth crystal on top of the fourth (middle) basil leaf.

2. Focus on the centre of the cross for a few moments, as you find stillness, and say, 'This cross of confidence empowers me with courage and autonomy. When I take the middle stone and leaf, I will be balanced and filled with a personal sense of empowerment.'

3. Take up the middle crystal with your writing hand and the basil leaf in your other hand and hold them in your fists, close to your navel. Imagine their power flowing through you and giving you the 'cross of life' – the ability to carry through your intention and a trusted belief in that intention. This is the union of spirit and matter (crystal and basil) that lies within you, enhancing trust in yourself.

4. Continue to hold the 'cross of life' to your belly for a minute or so, as you visualise inner integrity flowing through every part of your body, filling you with confidence.

5. When you feel ready, place the leaf on the table, but keep the crystal with you.

Whenever you feel a momentary wobble or lack of confidence, hold the stone tightly to your navel and it will reawaken your inner integrity.

Self-belief (and Belief)

Belief shapes our thoughts, actions and intentions. So if you believe in fairies, then you'll most likely encounter them; if you don't *truly* believe in them – well, then you won't. If you believe you are going to be a millionaire, and this belief is genuine, it will shape the way you act, think and live your life, until you become one.

Self-belief is about believing in who you are, being honest about your goals, your desires, needs and intentions. With this kind of integrity, anything you wish to happen will happen.

Of course, if you're a novice witch, then to start with you are working with blind faith, using other people's (or my) spells, so it's understandable you may not be thoroughly sure of the outcome. But with utter self-belief, and a belief in what you are doing, it will come true. Once you have had one successful outcome, however small or big, you can begin to adapt spells or write your own, if you prefer.

....

RITUAL TO PROMOTE SELF-BELIEF

This ritual empowers you with belief in yourself. Performing it at every new crescent moon will also restore your sense of purpose, if you find that it's diminishing at the end of a lunar cycle. I say this because the waning moon is a time of losing or letting go, when it can be hard to get a grip on your intentions and you might feel unmotivated, so sabotaging your self-esteem or belief system all over again.

You will need:
* A red rose
* Your journal or Book of Shadows

1. Hold a red rose to your third-eye chakra (see p. 283).

2. Close your eyes, relax and imagine 'passion' in the red petals; open yourself up not just to the abstract word, but to imagining and feeling passion, or visualise an image of a passionate kiss. Imagine this rose bringing you self-love, bestowing you with dedication, enthusiasm and motivational delight in who you are.

3. Focus on the flower's smell or its touch against your skin – the power of the rose's love filling you with serenity and self-belief.

4. When you feel ready, come out of your meditation on the rose, and place it in a safe place.

5. Gently pull off as many of the rose petals as you like and press them in your Book of Shadows or journal.

Open your book or journal to those pages whenever you have an inse-cure 'wobble'. You'll be reunited with the same empowering love of the rose and feel 'self-belief' flowing through you again.

Self-awareness

Before you discover how to focus, visualise or ask for what you seek, you need to be really aware of what you desire. Most of us think we know what we want, but we're often brainwashed by social, cultural or family beliefs and opin-ions. We think we want this or that car, more money or a different place to live, and that those things will make us happy. Remember, that great fortune you want may not be what you truly *need*, and it may not represent the authentic you.

....

RITUAL TO ENHANCE HONEST SELF-AWARENESS AND AUTHENTICITY

Use your journal, Book of Shadows or a piece of paper to record your thoughts about the following:

1. Think of the past:
   Think back to the happiest moment in your life. Write down what it was in as few words as possible. What were you doing at the time? Were you alone or with someone?
   Have you ever experienced an awe-inspiring or epiphany moment? If so, what did this experience feel like? Can you describe it?

What has given you meaning or purpose in life?

What has made you feel good to be you?

What has given you a sense of achievement?

2. Now think of the present:

What makes you frustrated or ill at ease at this point in your life?

What do you feel is lacking in your life?

Do you have any regrets? If so, what are they?

What makes you happy?

What would you love to do right now, this very minute? Even if you can't literally do this thing, can you now, this very moment, imagine or visualise yourself doing it? Write it down.

3. Now think of the future:

What would your ideal life be like? Describe it.

If you can imagine doing the thing you love the most now, can you see yourself doing it in the future? If you can't imagine it, what is blocking you?

What do you need to do, act, think or feel to have this in the future?

4. Look through your three lists and see if any 'themes' connect them. If there is a common element – whether an abstract concept, such as 'freedom', or a more tangible one, such as 'travel' or 'family' – this is a sign that you are beginning to sort out your true values from the meaningless ones.

Once you know what your true values are, and what truly matters to you, you can ask the universe to truly manifest this 'valued thing' to you. But you need to be honest about your feelings, too.

Care for Your Feelings

Being honest with yourself about your feelings can be hard. We are brought up to believe that we shouldn't have certain negative feelings, or at least not to reveal or project them on to other people. So while we might well have feelings of hate, anger, hurt and loss, what we should do with them is another matter.

To be a true manifesting witch, you need to accept that you have both positive and negative feelings and, in acknowledging them, know that you care about them and respect them for what they are: feelings.

....

RITUAL TO CARE FOR YOUR FEELINGS

The positive thoughts and feelings you identify in this ritual will help you to map out your intentions, as long as you are authentic about what you truly seek.

You will need:
* A pen and 2 pieces of paper

1. Below is a list of positive prompts and then a list of negative ones. Write out a list on each of your two pieces of paper, then complete the sentences as honestly as you can, adding as many words as you like for each prompt.

   List one:
   I wish . . .
   I enjoy . . .

I am grateful for . . .
I need . . .
I love receiving . . .
I love giving . . .
I am happiest when . . .

List two:
I hate . . .
I am most unhappy when . . .
I can't bear . . .
I get angry about . . .
I don't want . . .
My bad feelings arise when . . .
I don't like getting . . .
I don't like giving . . .

2. Think about the reactions and feelings that came to you when you wrote all this down. For example, did you feel hate when you wrote down the words, 'I hate . . .'? It's important that you are able to identify and experience these feelings or thoughts, simply because they are powerful qualities in you and common to us all. If you 'own' both negative and positive, you are taking the first steps towards flipping the negative into positive and taking control of your life to make appropriate choices.

   1. Now, focusing on the negatives first, admit to them and say: 'Welcome – you're not strangers, but I prefer to keep you out of my witch work. I do acknowledge you and will respect there are times I feel these things.'

   2. Fold up the piece of paper with the negative words on it and bury it in the garden or in a pot, or simply throw it in the bin to show you are not a prisoner of your negativity.

3. Next, take the list of positives and focus on them. Say the sentences over and over again, as if you are making affirmations; acknowledge these inner qualities and say, 'Welcome, you're not strangers, and I harness your goodness in my witch work'.

Keep the list of positives in your journal, Book of Shadows or on your altar and use it to check in with yourself whenever you feel a moment of doubt or negativity arise.

....

WHAT – MATTERS – TO – ME – NOW RITUAL

As its name suggests, this simple ritual will give you clarity about what matters to you right now. Then, when you start practising witch magic, you'll know you are doing it for you and you alone – the authentic you in this 'here and now'.

You will need:
* A jar with a lid
* A pen and paper
* Some lavender flowers (fresh or dried)

1. Find a jar or container with a lid (could be a jam jar). Whatever you choose, it is going to be your personal 'core-values' jar.

2. Make a list of ten or more of your values or things that matter to you. These could be ideas like 'freedom', 'kindness', 'strength' or 'fitness'. Choose as many as you like, then weed out those that don't truly 'sing to your heart' before committing to a final five.

3. Tear up a piece of paper into five small scraps and write on them the remaining five values that are important to you – things that truly matter to you right now. For example, you may place a high value on 'freedom', 'trust', 'security' or 'belonging'. Or it might be something more tangible, such as 'a roof over my head' or 'good health'.

4. Once you have determined your top five and have written them down, fold up the scraps of paper and place them in your jar.

5. Sprinkle over the lavender flowers (for purity of thought) to seal your intention. After twenty-four hours, open the jar, take in a deep whiff of the lavender perfume to cleanse and purify your mind, then scatter the flowers and papers on a table or the floor. Read your five values out loud, in no particular order. Intuitively, you will know which is the one you must aim to work into your life right now.

Acknowledging the need, desire or quality of your authentic self in this way is the first step to manifesting it.

What Is My Quest?

So what are you truly seeking? Is it a better lifestyle, health, love, wealth or spiritual contentment? It doesn't really matter what it is, as long as you are sure of your quest or goal.

....

WHAT – IS – MY – QUEST RITUAL

Once you have identified what matters most to you right now, you can shape it into something you can actually manifest and align it with positive intention.

You will need:
* A pen and paper

1. Write your quest down. Be specific about what you want and be positive. Visualise it; enter its space. Imagine you have it already. It's no good saying, 'I would like more money' (the word 'more' just means more than you have now, so it could be that you are rewarded with a penny more tomorrow than you have today). You need to specify exactly how much.

2. Are you someone who says things like, 'I never get' or, 'Why does this always happen to me?' If so, stop it now. Instead say, 'I always get what I desire' and, 'This is happening to me.' This suggests a more positive, proactive approach. By talking as if it *is* happening to you, rather than it *might*, you are aligning your energy with that of the cosmos.

Here are some positive affirmations to say aloud and also to write down and leave in places where you will see them every day. You might choose to look at them before you start any practice, to put yourself in a positive place:
* I know what I want and am dedicated to this intention.
* I trust the universe is bringing me what I desire.
* I am using the magic within me to manifest my goal.

* I believe, love and honour myself, and am true to my chosen destiny.
* My inner witch is the goodness in me.

With the self-understanding and dedication to your intentions you have acquired in this chapter, you can discover next how to harness the power of planets, deities and the sun and moon.

CHAPTER SIX

Working with the Luminaries, Planets and Deities

If you live in harmony with nature, you will never be poor; if you live according what others think, you will never be rich.
Seneca, ancient Roman Stoic philosopher

I n Wicca and all forms of witchcraft, the cycles of the sun, moon and planets are key elements for harnessing the energy of the cosmos and aligning to its power.

The Sun

In witchcraft, the transits of the sun and moon help to determine the best possible timings for casting spells. This follows the ancient belief that the energy harmoniously resonates with certain qualities at certain moments of the year, and also with the object of our intention, thus increasing the chances of its manifestation. For example, the summer solstice or Beltane would be the perfect times to cast love or commitment spells; and the spring equinox would work for romance or a new challenge. The sun, according to most Western traditions, is associated with the masculine archetype.

Throughout the year, the sun appears to move around the Earth along an imaginary belt known as the ecliptic. This path crosses lines of celestial longitude divided into twelve segments of 30°, forming a 360° circle. As the sun moves through these different segments, best known as the twelve signs of the zodiac, the energy subtly changes. For example, when the sun moves to 0° of Aries (marking the spring equinox), nature bursts into life, and there is growth, virility, activity and masculine energy; then, when the sun moves into Venus-ruled Taurus (around 20 May), the energy is more indulgent and pleasure loving.

....

RITUAL TO CONNECT TO THE SUN

You may often want to use the sun's empowering energy for your ritual spell work, so here's how to connect to its power, to show you have utter belief in its sunshiny magic.

1. On any sunny day (the sunnier, the better), at about midday, go outside, raise your face to the sky, close your eyes and open your arms out wide, as if to embrace the sun (never look directly at it).

2. Hold this position for a few rounds of deep breaths, as you take in the air and soak up the vitamin D and the natural energy flowing into and through you.

3. Next, do the same thing sitting cross-legged, only this time be aware of the earth beneath your sit bones, the sun beaming down on your face, and the power of its rays filling you with life.

4. Now lie down on the ground on your back (or, if this isn't possible, stand again) and repeat the above.

5. Return to a standing position (unless you're already in one) and say:

> Thank you, sun, for your gifts of light to me.
> For your golden chariot's pathway across the heavens,
> For the flowers that spring to life, for nature's energy.

6. When you feel ready to close down the ritual, simply drop your arms to your sides and bow graciously to the overhead sun.

You will feel vitalised and filled with the confidence to work with the sun in your craft.

The Moon

Traditionally, the moon's cycles have always been a key factor in timings for witchcraft. In ancient Greece, the dark goddess Hecate was linked with the dark of the moon and, some say, forbidden magic. Other goddesses associated with the moon were Artemis, who hunted by moonlight, and Selene, who enchanted the shepherd Endymion. The moon has long been identified with feminine energy and, in astrology, the moon represents our emotions, feelings, instincts and our ability to nurture. In fact, the physical moon has a powerful influence over the seas and tides and its changing phases are used as a guide by traditional gardeners.

For the modern witch, tracking the moon's path each month, or at least knowing when a full or new moon is due, means being able to use these phases to advantage. Either check them out in a current almanac or on the internet or get yourself an app or ephemeris (a chart showing the daily positions of the sun, moon and planets as they travel through the zodiac). If you're lucky enough, you may be able to see the moon waxing and waning in the sky. This kind of physical experience of moon-watching will help you to feel in touch with those powerful cycles, too.

New crescent/waxing-moon phase

This is the phase when you first start to glimpse the thinnest sliver of the light of the crescent moon curved outwards to the right in the northern hemisphere (to the left in the southern hemisphere). This usually lasts about a day, then it gradually waxes (grows bigger) until, approximately a week later, you will see the crescent become a semi-circle (the curve to the right in the northern hemisphere), then bigger and bigger, until it's a full moon (full circle, two weeks, approximately, after the new moon).

Use a new crescent moon and this waxing-moon phase to begin new projects, set new intentions, attract attention, get creative, be inspired to start any manifesting goals and generally start spell-casting. It is a great time to revive desire, prepare a new intention (however big or small) and get ready for a new adventure.

Full-moon phase

The full-moon phase is fairly obvious if you have a clear night. To check the actual moment of the full moon's culmination, you need to look in an ephemeris because it depends also where on Earth you are and at what time you may see it. But you don't have to be bang on accurate about its moment of culmination, as long as you are aware your intention is for a full-moon spell.

Use the phase just before and during the full moon for manifestation of commitment to your intention if you haven't already, and for finalising any spell work. It is a time for completion of any spells you might want to cast – it's now or never before the next cycle. You can also cast spells for commitment to a cause or a relationship, to seal a deal or ensure success with your plans.

Waning-moon phase

The moon begins to lose luminosity over the next two weeks, and diminishes in size, until you see a fine crescent curved out to the left in the northern hemisphere (to the right in the southern). As it slowly fades away, the waning moon is a time for reflection and release.

This is the perfect phase to perform banishing spells, freeing yourself from fears and emotions, simply letting go of the past, dropping self-imposed barriers and bringing clarity to what you truly want. It is a time for releasing bad feelings, but also honouring what has been and accepting the outcome. So in manifestation work, this can be called a 'reflective phase': think back on what you desired and why, and realise that what goes around comes around. In other words, if you put out good energy during the waxing- or full-moon phase, then recall that goodness will come back to you.

Dark-of-the-new-moon phase

This phase occurs over a couple of days around the exact conjunction of the sun and moon (i.e. when the sun and moon are aligned on the same side of the Earth, so the moon is not illuminated by the sun and therefore invisible to the eye). Once the conjunction has occurred, the next phase is the waxing new crescent moon.

Use this short dark-of-the-moon phase to retreat, reflect and repose. It's a time to dig deep and know what you truly want. Only perform spells concerned with opening up your mind to possibilities, but not for intention or goal setting. This is a time for renewing contact with and dedication to your inner witch, thus acknowledging and honouring the hidden potentials within you. It is also a time for performing rituals to nurture your deepest values, desires and needs.

The new crescent moon starts the cycle again, heralding the waxing phase.

RITUAL TO CONNECT TO THE MOON

Before working with the moon, give blessings to the moon goddess, and show her your intention to draw on her power.

You can choose any of the lunar phases to establish a lunar connection. It's entirely up to you, but just be aware of which phase it is, and adapt the following words accordingly, to make it clear you are in tune with the moon.

You will need:

* A mirror
* A glass of water
* A silver ring, coin or other small silver object

1. As the sun sets, take your mirror, glass of water and chosen silver object (all attributes of the moon) and place them outside, somewhere you can sit for a few minutes in reflection.

2. Turn the mirror face down and drop the silver object into the glass of water.

3. Hold the glass up to the sky and say the following (dropping in the relevant word for the phase of the moon you're in: waxing/fullness/waning/darkness):

> Oh, lunar phase of [. . .] bright,
> I welcome now your silver light.
> To send me trust and fair moonbeams
> And call upon you for my dreams.

4. Now turn the mirror face up and place the glass of water in the middle of it to reflect the moon and draw on her power.

5. Leave the mirror and glass in place overnight.

In the morning, look down at yourself through the now moon-empowered water and into the mirror, and you will be connected to the moon's loving energy whenever you need to work with moon magic.

Planets

In astrology and many other esoteric arts, the planets are thought to exert an influence over us (symbolically or otherwise) and are identified with deities the world over. Each radiates its own magical power through its position in the sky and its symbolic resonance. In astrology, the patterns the planets make in the sky as they travel around the ecliptic (the apparent pathway of the sun) are drawn up as a 'horoscope'. This is a 'map' of the planets' positions at any moment in time, and can reflect an event, a person or an individual born into that moment to reveal their qualities.

We can draw on the symbolic power of these planets, just as we can their associated deities.

Mercury

Mercury orbits the sun so fast that one year on Mercury is the equivalent of eighty-eight Earth days. (A planet's year is calculated by the time it takes to orbit once around the sun.)

So if you lived on Mercury, you'd have a birthday approximately every three months. Mercury's eccentric behaviour is called upon to promote clever thoughts and inspire quirky or off-the-wall manifestation goals.

Venus

Situated between Mercury and the Earth, Venus is hotter than Mercury, although further away from the sun, and is often thought to be Earth's twin, with similar size, composition and density. Exceptionally bright, it is known as, and appears as, both the morning and evening star. After the sun and moon, it is the most brilliant body in the sky. Venus is the perfect planet to manifest goals to do with art, aesthetics, beauty, values, sensuality and harmony; and it has well-known associations with love, named, as it is, after the Roman goddess of love, Venus.

Mars

The planet Mars, between Earth and Jupiter, usually appears red, due to the amount of iron on its surface. Like its namesake, the god Mars, its magical associations are about challenge, conflict and impulsiveness, but when called upon in spell work it can promote dynamic action and pioneering ideas.

Jupiter

The planet Jupiter is named after Zeus' Roman counterpart and is the largest in the solar system (after the sun). In magic,

Jupiter's energy is concerned not only with excitement and action, but also optimism, joie de vivre, manifesting truth, justice, business and wealth.

Saturn

Saturn was the furthest known planet in the ancient world. (Uranus and Neptune were not discovered until the eighteenth and twentieth centuries, respectively.) Saturn can be called upon in magic spells to help manifest affairs concerned with the law, individual integrity, responsibility, duty, family and home security.

Uranus

Surrounded by a gang of twenty-seven known moons, this cold and windy planet was unknown by the ancient seers and sorcerers, and not discovered until the eighteenth century. It is associated with radical thinking, eccentricity, reform, humanitarian and global ideas, and can be drawn on to help manifest innovative concepts and sudden change.

Neptune

Even colder than Uranus, this ice giant has supersonic winds, and is invisible from Earth, a testament to its numinous power. In astrology, it is associated with the sea, intuition, illusion, fantasy, dreams, art and magic. You can draw on Neptune's power for creative inspiration, but this planet is less concerned with 'reality' than the others, and its purpose is to manifest dreams into thought, so that thought can then be put into action via other spell work.

Pluto

Pluto is considered a planet in some astrological circles, but in astronomical terms it has been reclassified as a 'dwarf planet'. Whatever the case, its symbolic influence is thought to include power, control, transformation and anything dark, taboo or off limits. Calling on Pluto will encourage power into your life – but only do so with an intention to bring positive change for yourself and others, or you may find others trying to control you.

The Planets and the Magical Power of Numbers

We take numbers for granted. Like the letters of an alphabet, we see them all around us, and forget that they too are symbols, and not simply useful devices for our calculated, measured, engineered world.

Numbers are of huge importance in our mystical, magical world. A particular number of things occur frequently in spells – the number of candles, repetitions of a verse, ingredients and so on. These symbols are more potent than you might imagine, and are believed to have their own magical, universal power.

Ancient cultures – from the ancient Chinese and Babylonians to the Egyptians – believed in the power of numbers, but for our purposes the belief system most commonly used in Western magic, and on which the mystical art of numerology is based, is that of the ancient Greek philosopher and mathematician Pythagoras.

Pythagoras wrote that 'numbers are the first things of all nature'. He believed they were the key to the workings of the universe and cosmic wisdom. He also theorised that each of the one-digit numbers (one to nine) vibrates to a specific frequency, and these vibrations echo through the universe. He called this 'the music of the spheres', played by the heavenly bodies (the known planets at the time), each with their own numerical value and harmonic vibration. Later, the sixteenth- and seventeenth-century German astrologer and astronomer Johannes Kepler developed this idea and called this 'music' 'a continuous song for several voices'. Simply put, Kepler believed the planets emit their own unique harmonics, due to their elliptical orbits, creating a musical harmony of the 'spheres' (i.e. planets), which only our souls can hear. So when we sing or speak in rhythms that are in harmony with the cosmos, we are more powerfully aligned to this *musica universalis*. If we could 'sing' along to these musical vibrations using numbers, therefore, we could invoke the power of the planets for our own use.

Here is a brief guide to the qualities associated with numbers one to nine, suggesting how you might use them in spells and witchcraft:

* One – action, innovation and independence

* Two – negotiation, adaptability, co-operation

* Three – communication, relationship, engagement

* Four – realism, practicality, achievement, production

* Five – questioning, exploration, creativity, self-expression

* Six – protection, service, construction, classification

* Seven – mysticism, intuition, spontaneity, adventure

* Eight – ambition, determination, materialism, power

* Nine – vision, goal setting, success, manifestation

....

RITUAL TO CONNECT TO THE PLANETS AND THE MUSIC OF THE SPHERES

As the musical vibration of numbers is orchestrated by the planets, here's how to get in tune with the planets and the 'music of the spheres'. Try this on a pleasant day, when you feel ready to connect to the heavenly bodies.

1. Find a quiet, comfortable place, preferably outside. Raise your face and look at the sky.

2. For a few moments, think about how the Earth revolves around the sun, as do the planets, yet we have this fundamental perception of a

geocentric world view in which the sun revolves around us. (Rather like the ego, or perception of oneself – the world 'appears' to revolve around us.)

3. Now, turn your attention to the sky. Imagine the planets singing their own melodies but all in harmony, like a great operatic performance. You want to reach out to them, to participate in their music – so start to hum, sing or chant a tune that you love. It can just be a riff or verse from a popular song, a nursery rhyme with words, a few lines from a well-known pop song, a piece of classical music or just a scale – anything that you find yourself singing with joy in your heart.

4. Repeat your chosen melody nine times (nine is the number of manifestation and magic), then take a few moments' calm.

5. Repeat the melody again nine times, and then take another few moments' calm.

6. Repeat another nine times. This way, you have sung with the *musica universalis* and woven your soul's tune into the cosmic opus.

7. Thank the planets for being in harmony with you.

Now, whenever you want to 'tune in' to the power of the planets and their musical values, just hum your chosen song or sing it in your head and feel connected.

Deities

There are pantheons (collections) of deities the world over, so it's really down to personal choice as to which you feel an affinity with – if any. If you're not born into the culture associated with your chosen deities, don't worry, but take care that you are not disrespectful of the belief system and that you honour its tradition. There are also hosts of local spirits, lares (household spirits), nymphs, fairies, other-worldly entities and so on to draw on from different magic and belief systems. Whatever the case, all divine entities can help to manifest your goals should you choose to call on them.

Wiccan deities

In Wicca, the generic names for the two main deities are the God and the Goddess, and the most common names for them are the Horned God and the Earth Goddess. The Earth Goddess is also known as the Triple Goddess – maiden, mother, crone – or just the Goddess. Wiccans often call on other deities from a wide variety of polytheistic traditions, depending on personal choice.

Horned God

The Horned God lives in the forests, woods and natural wild and is usually the consort or lover of the Goddess. The seasonal cycle, the Wheel of the Year, is often marked by the relationship between the Horned God and the Goddess (although they are also known as the sun god and the

Goddess). According to some Wiccans, the Horned (or sun) God is born in winter, mates with the fertile Goddess in spring and then dies during the autumn months, to be given birth to by the Goddess at Yule again. The god is also identified with the Oak King in the summer and the Holly King in the winter. In traditional Wicca, the Horned God is generally regarded as a dualistic god of light and dark, night and day, summer and winter.

The Goddess

Again, confusion can arise here, as different Wiccan groups talk about the Triple Goddess or Maiden, Mother, Crone, as well as the Earth Goddess or simply the Great Goddess of ancient Neolithic times. So it's up to you whether you choose to call on the Goddess and the Horned God or any one of the deities I've used in this book.

Greek deities

Probably the best known pantheon in Western mythology, the ancient Greek gods and goddesses have always been associated with magic work.

Zeus

Zeus was the ruler of the skies in Greek mythology, associated with thunder and lightning and renowned for his seductive power. He fathered many other gods (he was promiscuous and had both divine and mortal lovers), including Artemis, Apollo, Athene and Hermes. In magic work, he is called on for help in both love and success spells, his boundless yet sometimes zealous energy invoking change and excitement.

Aphrodite

The goddess of love, sexuality, beauty and vanity, Aphrodite is renowned for her turbulent affairs with Ares, the god of war (with whom she parented the god of passion and lust, Eros) and the mortal Adonis, killed by a boar (a jealous Ares). She is called upon for all types of love and romance magic, while her association with doves manifests peace and harmony in the home and her links with roses and myrtle bring happiness to all who favour her.

Hermes

The god of trade, trickery and magic, Hermes moved freely between the divine and mortal worlds. As a messenger of the gods, he was also associated with the wind, boundaries and travel. In magic spells, he is called upon to help manifest better communication and clarity of thought and writing, to channel inspiration and creativity and to aid travel.

Cronus

Cronus was the first of the so-called Titans and the son of Gaia (Mother Earth) and Ouranos, the sky god. He over-threw Ouranos, but was later overthrown, in turn, by his own son Zeus. He became assimilated into the Roman pantheon as the god Saturn, and both can be called upon for spells requiring protection, discipline, order, good timing and property matters.

Ares

The god of war, Ares stormed around the place looking for trouble, especially after he was caught red-handed in a clandestine embrace with his lover, Aphrodite. Hephaestus (Aphrodite's husband) strung them up in a net, so that all the gods could laugh at them. Ares may have been a bit of brute on one level, but he was an honourable god of war, and represents our drive, willpower, impulse, initiative and the way we get things done. He's called upon to promote action and initiative in any manifesting spell.

Helios

Sun god, Helios, drove his golden chariot across the skies by day, and is best known for the problems he had with his son Phaeton who, wanting to prove his worth, impetuously took the reins of his father's chariot, but lost control and plummeted close to the world, setting it alight. To save the Earth, Zeus struck him dead with a lightning bolt. In another tale, Helios' affair with the mortal princess Leucothoe led to her demise. To prevent her body from rotting in the ground, he turned her into a frankincense tree, the aromatic oil from which was subsequently used in Helios' worship. We can call upon Helios and use sacred frankincense to illuminate our desires and fire them into action.

Selene

The moon goddess, Selene, was the sister of Helios and Eos (the dawn). She was later identified with Artemis and Hecate, and possibly part of the first moon goddess triad. She is best known for enchanting the mortal shepherd Endymion into an eternal sleep, so that she could come down at night and make love to him. Although not worshipped as openly as the other gods, Selene had subtler cult followings, but became associated with doom-laden eclipses and the darker doings of witchcraft. In popular folk magic, however, she was called upon for love, fertility and childbirth spells.

....

RITUAL TO CONNECT TO A CHOSEN DEITY OR SPIRIT

When you choose a deity to help you with your magic, you first need to connect to them and show your gratitude. Do the following ritual once you have identified a favourite god or goddess and you want to call on their aid for your spell work (or just for moments of serenity and comfort).

1. Decorate or dress your altar or sacred space with appropriate motifs or attributes associated with the deity. Perhaps prop up a mirror as a symbol of your 'portal' into the spirit world. Light candles to add atmosphere, and check out associations of the days, seasons, sabbats or moon phases that align to your chosen deity, so you can experience a deeper connection.

107

2. Call on your deity in a simple, kindly way. For example: 'I call on you, Great Goddess, for help and encouragement to manifest my intentions. Thank you for your presence and please grant me your protection and guidance in my quest.'

3. Show gratitude and honour by offering fruit, flowers or an appropriate crystal and leave these on your 'altar' to give thanks and blessing.

Once you have done this, you will be able to connect to the deity of your choice just by asking for their blessing and help.

Whichever deity, planet, solar or lunar phase you choose to work with, they are there to enrich your spells and intentions.

Next, we're going to look at the power of symbols and how they too can enhance your craft.

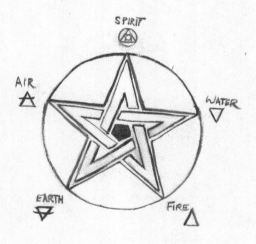

CHAPTER SEVEN

Working with Symbols and Signs

A symbol is indeed the only possible expression of some invisible essence, a transparent lamp about a spiritual flame . . .
W. B. Yeats, Irish poet and writer

A symbol is a visual image representing something else, such as an abstract idea, a hidden message or a universal truth. We use symbols every day in the form of numbers, letters, street signs, colours or codes, whether to transmit messages or to disclose secret information. The word 'symbol' derives from the Greek word '*symballein*', meaning 'to throw or cast together'. When we see a symbol, we usually (and often unconsciously) recognise its meaning. For example, most of us connect the familiar motif of a rose with love, and the colour red with passion.

The symbols used in this book, whether astrological, magical or otherwise, are a form of language that will help you to connect to the power of the universe.

Some have specific designs or geometrical patterns and often impart a hidden or esoteric meaning, shared only by those in the know. These are mostly evident among secret societies, such as the Rosicrucians or Freemasons, whose messages are intended only for the initiated.

In Wicca and witchcraft, the most important symbols are the pentagram and pentacle (a pentagram with a circle drawn around it), the Triple Goddess, the Horned God, the four seasons, the five magic elements and the witch's knot. These are not only protective symbols, but can also strengthen and enhance your connection to the positive energy around you.

The Pentagram

A protective symbol against negativity and unwanted psychic or geopathic energy, the pentagram is used in spells to focus and align to the power of the five elements (as represented by each point of the star): Earth, Air, Fire, Water and Spirit. In some traditions, the elements also represent love, wisdom, law, knowledge and power.

The Wiccan pentagram is usually drawn with the top point of the star pointing north, although this can be reversed. When the main point is pointing south (called an inverted pentagram), it is usually identified with black or satanic magic.

Awakening to the power of the pentagram

To connect to the pentagram, try drawing one without taking your pen off the paper. (Drawing one continuous line is thought to represent the infinity of the universe – much as when we draw a perfect circle, we form a never-ending cycle of life.) Practise drawing a pentagram on paper – then when you want to cast a symbol of protective power before performing any spell, you can simply trace it in the air with your finger. Here's how:

You will need:
* A pen and paper

1. Starting at the top point, draw a slightly angled line down to mark the bottom right point.

2. Keeping your pen on the paper, draw a slightly angled line up to make the top left point opposite.

3. Take the pen straight across from here, horizontally, to mark the top right point.

4. Keeping pen on paper all the while, draw a diagonal line down to the left to mark the bottom left point.

5. Finally, draw a diagonal line back up to meet the top point you started from.

Once you get the hang of drawing these, you can use pentagrams to decorate your altar, sanctuary or wherever you feel appropriate (say, the front cover of your journal or Book of Shadows). You could also make a pentagram mobile out of craft paper and hang it in your window to welcome the magic of the cosmos. You will find pentagrams in many of the spells in Part Two.

PENTAGRAM EMPOWERMENT RITUAL

♡

Try this ritual to feel your inner witch come alive.

You will need:
* A pen and paper

1. Draw a perfect pentagram on your piece of paper.

2. Write your name (the one you prefer to be known by) in each of the points, and the word 'magic' in the centre.

3. Focus on your drawing for a moment, and repeat five times: 'I am [your preferred name], and I am magic, too.'

Repeat the above to awaken pentagram power within you whenever you're struggling to feel it.

The Five Elements

The elements are magic forces associated with the five points of the pentagram.

The five elements are thought to be the building blocks of the universe. They occur within many world esoteric belief systems, including Chinese, Ayurvedic and Vedic teachings, and are known by different names. In Chinese astrology, for example, they are known as Fire, Earth, Water, Metal and Wood.

In Western magic traditions, they are usually identified with the four elements of astrology (Fire, Earth, Air and Water) and the fifth element, spirit, is thought to be the universe – the divine itself or one's own soul. After all, the divine flows through you, doesn't it?

PENTACLES IN TAROT

Arthur Edward Waite, one of the founding members of the late nineteenth-century British esoteric group the Hermetic Order of the Golden Dawn, is renowned for developing the Rider–Waite–Smith tarot deck. The pentagram appears in the deck as the suit of pentacles. In tarot, pentacles (also known as coins) represent earth, wands symbolise Fire, swords signify Air and cups Water.

In our witchcraft pentagram, 'Spirit' is considered to be at the top of the star, controlling the four elements, aligning to the four winds and quarters (the compass directions) and their associated spiritual energies.

Fire (south)

Passion, action, courage, willpower, illumination, career, goal setting, travel

Associated with the sun and the astrological Fire signs, Aries, Leo and Sagittarius, Fire is the quality we need to be motivated and dynamic and gives us impetus and impulse to start our quest. Fire corresponds to red and orange, and is often symbolised in magic work with candles, incense and red crystals.

Earth (north)

Strength, achievement, material success, determination, practical creativity

Connected to the astrological signs of Taurus, Virgo and Capricorn, Earth describes the tangible world, the practical aspects of our lives and how we work on a daily basis. It represents abundance, pleasure, worldly indulgence and all the materialistic aspects of living. In magic, it is symbolised by the colour green and by nature's gifts, such as plants, herbs, rocks, crystals and wood.

Air (east)

Inspiration, intellect, communication, understanding, logic, wisdom, language

Air is about creative thinking, the intellect, the way we interact, how we think of ourselves and others, not forgetting our beliefs and our perception of the world around us. The Air signs are Gemini, Libra and Aquarius, and its colours are yellow and white. Air is represented in magic work with abstract symbols, such as the pentagram, incantations, mantras, affirmations and divination methods.

Water (west)

Intuition, feelings, emotions, spiritual healing, imagination, music, art

Water is the instinct, emotion and feelings of both the individual and the collective, drawing on the spiritual and the numinous. The Water signs are Cancer, Scorpio and

Pisces. Water motifs and spells take us into the unknown and the unconscious. It is the element that can heal and nurture us, protecting us from psychic pollution. For spell work, Water is symbolised by the colours blue and black, not forgetting the moon and actual water or the ocean itself.

Spirit (you)

All qualities

The quintessential element is, of course, you. If the divine or the universe flows through all things, then it flows through you, too, and is your spirit or soul. Spirit is all of yourself, your dreams, your qualities, your hidden potentials, your inner witch and your deepest sacred self.

....

RITUAL FOR BEING INSPIRED BY THE ELEMENTS

Whether it's a sunny, sparkling, chilly, breezy, balmy or just a calm and comforting day, step outside and embrace the five elements. All it takes is to engage with each of them, and experience and be inspired by their energies.

1. **First engage with Fire energy:** you don't have to light a fire – simply watch the sun rise or sun set. The sun is Fire at its most intense and, as such, it can burn your skin, so midday is not the time to engage with its harmful rays – but when the sun is rising or setting, you can

enjoy its power and maximise it to your advantage without getting 'scorched'.

Sit and watch the sun as it rises or falls over the horizon. Reflect on how Fire not only brings warmth, but also lightens our way. Maybe notice the changes in sunlight throughout one day, and write your impressions in your journal. Reflect on how the sun colours the sky, brings passion to the landscape and adds dramatic touches of golden light to every leaf, twig, bird or your skin.

We are heated by Fire, but its energy ignites our passion, too, and enlightens our thoughts, opening our minds to new challenges and possibilities.

2. **Next, engage with the Earth:** literally push your hand into some soft soil. Or, if that's not a possibility, run your fingers through some soft greenery and feel the sensation of all that is tactile and tangible. Earth energy grounds us, so sit on the ground and imagine you are rooted to it; feel your sit bones connected to the deepest bones of the Earth, with all its treasures of crystals, minerals, gemstones and the ever-changing crust around its iron core. Reflect on how you are part of this Earth energy, too, and how everything on this planet, including yourself, is infused with the animating force of the universe.

3. **Now engage with Air:** look up at the skies. Watch the clouds, see birds flying high and spot distant satellites or even the moon, if it's dusk or later. Take a deep breath of air and imagine it filling not only your lungs, but your heart and soul, too, with the one thing that breathes life into you – precious oxygen. We all share this air. For example, think of our symbiotic relationship with trees. We breathe out carbon dioxide, trees 'breathe' it in; they 'breathe out'

oxygen which we breathe in to survive. Respecting this thing called Air means you will begin to respect all of life which depends on it, too.

4. **Next, engage with Water:** if you have the time, find a stretch of water – the sea, a lake, a river, stream or even a pond. If you are unable to fulfil this part of the ritual, however, simply fill a bowl with spring water. Swirl your toes or your fingers in your chosen body of water – whether the surf, the trickling stream, still lake or your bowl. Look at how the water reflects the sky, overhanging trees or maybe your own face, then gaze down and perhaps see fish, shells, rocks or currents. You may see shapes and shadows, nymphs and gods, and the watery power of the depths of yourself. When you begin to notice the myriad patterns, colours, shapes and even otherworldly beings in water, think how they are all reflecting aspects of you, too.

5. **Finally, engage with Spirit – with *you*:** be kind to yourself. Meditate on your goodness, your qualities, your desires and dreams. Take time – maybe an hour or even just five minutes, any day, every day or just when you feel the moment is right to awaken authenticity. Step out of the outer layer of your ostensible self and engage with the real you – the one with utter belief in your goals and your purpose – and ask yourself: what gives you meaning in life right now? And know that you can give life to those dreams through your magical craft.

The Circle

The circle is a symbol of completion, oneness or wholeness. It can be drawn on paper and filled with ideas or images to create a powerful mandala.

In witchcraft, you can use the circle in a tangible way to help you manifest your goals. Casting a circle around you means you are separated and protected from any negativity from the outside world. You can then work your magic from inside this sacred space, wherever you are. The magic circle also invites the positive energy of the elements, four directions and spiritual entities to come into your circle and help you achieve your aim, while protecting you from unwanted psychic or geopathic stress.

Casting a magic circle

All you need for this is yourself and your finger, but you can use a stick, rod, candle, flower, pencil or any other pointed prop you like to evoke the symbol of a wand. In some of the spells in this book, I mention scattering a circle of flowers around you or laying a grid of crystals – these are extra reinforcements that can also create a deeper protective element for your intention.

1. The sun rises in the east, making this the favoured direction from which to begin your circle. So start by facing east in your chosen spot, with enough space around you to swirl around.

2. Hold out the index finger of your writing hand (or your wand or stick) and, pointing to the east, say, 'I send blessings and thanks to the east to protect and help me in my spell.'

3. Turn anti-clockwise to the south and repeat the same words (substituting south for east, obviously).

4. Turn again, to the west and the north, respectively, repeating the words each time.

5. Return to the east again and say, 'Thank you spirits and winds of the east for your protection.'

6. Turn clockwise now, and repeat the words (again, substituting the direction at each compass point), until you are once again facing east.

Your circle of protection is now complete, and you can perform your spell in complete safety.

Triple Goddess

The Wiccan Triple Goddess symbol describes three phases of the moon, also corresponding to the three phases of life. The triad is known as Maiden, Mother and Crone, and represents the human life cycle (youthful vigour, nurturing mother and wise elder) and that of all life. In some traditions, the triad symbolises three specific Greek goddesses – Persephone (Maiden), Demeter (Mother) and Hecate (Crone).

In Wiccan lore, the Triple Goddess is lover of all, yet she is wed to none and is an embodiment of the sacred feminine archetype. She can also appear in many emanations, such as the Greek moon goddess, Selene, Isis, the Egyptian goddess of magic and motherhood or Diana, goddess of the hunt. They all represent various aspects of the stages of womanhood and are interwoven within the creative energy of the moon.

The waxing moon relates to maidenhood – a time of fresh innocence, of vitality and seductive power; the full moon relates to Mother, the power of fertility, protection, inner sanctity and nurturing; and the waning moon correlates with the Crone or older woman and her wisdom, age and experience, as she moves towards the dark-of-the-moon period and the rebirth of the Maiden.

This symbol is used in manifesting spells to promote all forms of creativity and to capture the essence of these three lunar cycles, thus tripling the spell's power.

RITUAL TO CONNECT TO THE TRIPLE GODDESS

This ritual will encourage you to understand the three energies of the Triple Goddess symbol and how they are reflected in the lunar cycle.

You will need:
* A pen and paper

1. On the day of a waxing moon, draw a Triple Goddess symbol (you can find one online or refer to the illustration on p. 00).

2. In the waxing-crescent-moon section, write a short-term intention (such as 'declutter wardrobe'), then in the full-moon section fill in a deadline for doing so and, in the waning-crescent-moon section, your intended result. (The first moon relates to creation, the middle to activating your intention and the last to the outcome.)

3. Once you have filled in your three sections, say:

> With triple-moon intentions met
> From first-moon thought I start the bet,
> With full moon bright I seal the pact,
> When last moon fades, I end this act.

Work with the phases of the moon to act out your written intention and to experience how this powerful symbol reflects the growth, formation and manifestation of any spell work.

Horned God

The Horned God is wild, sexual, magical and the masculine archetype of the life force. Believed to inhabit the woods, forests and nature, he is the symbol of the wilderness in us all. In Greek mythology he is likened to Pan; in English and Welsh folklore, he is respectively the gods Herne and Bran. In the Wiccan wheel of the year, the Horned God (aka the sun god) dies each autumn and is reborn at Yule, becoming virile in spring, then coupling again with the goddess in the summer, so repeating the cycle of the seasons.

When the symbols of the Horned God and the Triple Goddess are used together, the union of the sacred feminine and masculine archetypes create a divine wholeness and the most magical of qualities – the power of love. Used in spells the goddess and Horned God can be called on to stabilise relationship or marriage problems or bring harmony to the home.

RITUAL TO CONNECT TO THE HORNED GOD

Here's a simple ritual to help you understand the energy behind the Horned God symbol.

You will need:
* A pen and paper
* Some glue

1. Draw the Horned God symbol (see illustration, p. 00).

2. In the circle, write down three wild animals you love. Think carefully – could you love a badger, a fox, a wolf or a lion? Which three animals 'speak to you'? In other words, which do you identify with mostly, or perhaps wish you were?

(If you don't identify with or feel you could love any animal, you can also choose from any form of natural life, including trees and other botanicals.)

3. Once you have made your choice – and you can take your time with this, over a number of hours or days – and you have written the animals down, find an image of each one (or if you're artistic, you can draw them yourself) and glue (or simply place) your Horned God symbol below them.

4. Now say, 'With the wild at my side, I am potent, alive. This symbol my guide in the forest of life.'

Keep your symbol on display, alongside your Triple Goddess, to remind you always of their dual power: nurturing, cyclical and changing (the Goddess) and potent, active and procreative (the God).

Witch's Knot

Also known as the 'witch's charm' or 'magical charm', this symbol, like the pentagram, can be drawn in a continuous line without lifting pen from paper. (If you practise enough, you will be able to do it.)

Like the circle and the five-pointed star, the knot promotes protection and 'binding' power to your desired intention – whatever it is. Although it is usually used as an image, you can actually tie this knot with a piece of cord or ribbon to create an even more powerful binding spell. Once the charm has manifested your desired goal, you should cut or untie the knot to release the positive energy back to the universe.

....

RITUAL TO DRAW ON THE POWER OF THE WITCH'S KNOT

This ritual will enable you to draw the witch's knot whenever you need to include it in a spell.

You will need:
* A pen and paper (or an image of a knot)

1. Draw your own knot on a piece of paper (or use an image of one that you like; (there are different versions online, so choose the design that you like best or copy the illustration on p. 274).

2. Slowly trace your finger along the knot in one continuous line and, as you do so, repeat three times, 'I use this knot as tied to my intention, and to protect my pathway.'

You are now connected to the power of the witch's knot, which will help to protect you and your intention when casting any spell.

There are many other symbols you could use in magic work, such as astrological glyphs and alchemical signs, but the selection I've given you here will get you off to a great start. The next chapter looks at the powerful influences of the seasons of the witch.

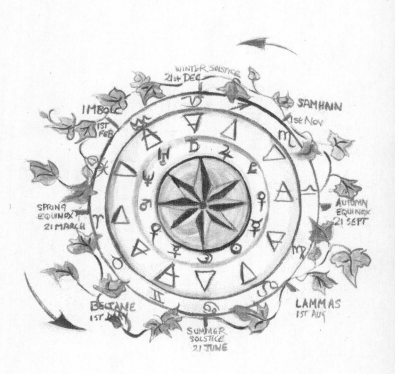

CHAPTER EIGHT

Seasons of the Witch

And Spring arose on the garden fair,
Like the Spirit of Love felt everywhere;
And each flower and herb on Earth's dark breast
Rose from the dreams of its wintry rest.
Percy Bysshe Shelley, English poet

There are times in the year that are key moments for both celebrating your dedication to being a modern witch and casting manifestation spells.

Working with the Seasons

The wheel of the year is a seasonal cycle of eight festivals marking the eternal cycle of growth and rebirth. These celebrations, known as sabbats, follow a nature-based calendar and include four solar festivals and four 'seasonal' ones. These are times for reflection, celebration and consolidation – a time to break free from the everyday stresses of modern living, join in the festivity and embrace change.

The most commonly known sabbats are:

* Winter solstice (Yule) – around 21 December

* Imbolc – 1/2 February

* Spring equinox (Ostara) – around 21 March

* Beltane – 30 April/1 May

* Summer solstice (Litha) – around 21 June

* Lammas – 1/2 August

* Autumn equinox (Mabon) – around 21 September

* Samhain – 31 October/1 November

Because the cycle is, of course, never-ending, the wheel of the year can start at different points in the year, according to various neopagan traditions. For example, some Wiccans prefer to use Samhain to mark the end and beginning of the year (associated with the last harvest), while others believe the winter solstice marks the end and beginning, as the sun begins to climb high in the sky again. It's up to you to make a choice as to whether you prefer one over the other. They are all beginnings and endings in themselves, so for the purposes of this book I'm going to begin with the winter solstice.

Winter solstice/Yule (c. 21 December)

When the sun arrives at 0° Capricorn, this marks the beginning of the shortest day in the northern hemisphere. Gradually, the sun begins to climb towards its zenith and the summer solstice. During Yule, there is a sense of stillness. Winter in the northern hemisphere is usually cold, but can be mildly grey, wet, dull, crisp or freezing and bleak. We feel a change in the air, too, as nature downs tools for a while, holing up for its winter break. The pagan Yule festival celebrates the coming of more daylight, with the death of the old sun god and the goddess who now gives birth to the sun king. Trees are decorated in his honour, and Yule logs are burned in the fireplace to protect the home and bring good luck for the coming year.

Best for: nestling into a cosy sharing of gratitude and giving with friends and family. (This relates to Christmas, too.) Show your love for others, and don't expect anything in return. This is the time for the modern witch to write down plans for the coming calendar year, whether related to personal development, romantic intentions or big ambitions. Although it's a seasonal time for reflection, celebration and revival, any spell work performed is suited to setting new resolutions for the future, preparation for long-term investment, career opportunities or commitment to a personal cause.

Imbolc (1/2 February)

Also known as Candlemas and St Brigid's Day, Imbolc celebrates the early signs of spring, when bluebells and celandine rise up through the dark earth. The goddess is also reborn in her new role of maiden and, like Persephone, she walks again on the upper earth, bringing it to life, so that the ground is ready for planting out seeds and we begin to enjoy the longer, lighter days. She does not yet know that she will soon be meeting the youthful sun god (or Horned God), who is learning his art of procreation deep within the wild woods. Imbolc is also associated with the Celtic goddess Brigid, also known as Bride, the goddess of sacred wells and fertility. Brigid dolls and crosses (made from the previous year's sheaves of corn) were traditionally placed in the home at this time for luck and love.

Best for: this is the perfect time for performing rituals to show your complete devotion to participating in the natural world. You can also use this time to reaffirm your belief and trust in your inner witch. If you set any resolutions during Yule, you can now start to put them into practice. For example, take a grounding crystal (such as black tourmaline) and plant it beneath a tree to show your dedication to your future, and make a Brigid cross (see above) to protect the home. With the sun now in Aquarius, perform spells for humanitarian or ecological innovation.

Spring equinox/Ostara
(c. 21 March, northern hemisphere)

The spring (or vernal) equinox marks a time of renewal, the bursting forth of plant and animal life; and, with the sun directly over the equator, day and night are of (almost) equal length across the world. Wiccans and pagans celebrate and give thanks to the Anglo-Saxon goddess of the dawn and personification of spring, Eostre, also known as Ostara. Birds begin to sing again, and we spend more time outside feeling the warmth of the sun on our faces. So let Ostara welcome you to your personal springtime.

Best for: the first day of the equinox, as the sun moves to 0° of swift-paced Aries, is perfect for 'fast-track' manifestation spells, whether seizing new opportunities, making new contacts, finding a new life direction or empowering yourself with the spirit of adventure. Use this moment of equality and balance to declutter, spring clean and bring harmony and fresh positivity into your home.

Beltane (1 May, northern hemisphere)

Falling midway between the spring equinox and the summer solstice, on the eve and first day of May, this ancient pagan festival celebrates fertility. Bonfires were traditionally lit in honour of the Celtic god Belenus (also known as Bel, the bright one) to ensure his protection of cattle put out to the summer pastures. To Wiccans, Beltane (meaning 'bright fire') is a celebration of the marriage of the Goddess and the sun god (or Horned God). It is a time when hedgerows and waysides are clouded with hawthorn blossom and love and romance are in the air. There's a sense of liberation and joy. Phallic maypoles, fire festivals and Morris dancers promote the fertility theme. Bees begin to buzz, tadpoles resemble tiny frogs in sparkling ponds and the countryside glistens with early dawn dew.

Best for: this is the perfect time to collect charms, crystals, symbols, flowers and motifs associated with love and romance and for writing love spells, perhaps to be used in the days or months ahead. It's also a cycle for loving yourself more, attending to your sensual needs and casting spells for romance and commitment. If you intend to do any manifesting spells at this time, focus on love and sensuality. Beltane falls mid-Taurus – a sign of pleasure, its ruler is Venus, the goddess of love and seduction. This is a time for merriment and light-hearted self-indulgence, so celebrate and enjoy the Beltane fun.

The Summer solstice/Litha (c. 21 June, northern hemisphere)

The summer solstice of 21 June (in the northern hemisphere), also known as Litha since the 1970s, is marked by the sun's move to 0° Cancer and the height of the solar god's ultimate power. This time is all about abundance, growing crops and welcoming the long, hot days of the coming summer. Bonfires and beacons were traditionally lit on high ground, not only to bring luck and protect the coming harvest, but also to signal the sun's power, when the days are longest and the sun has reached its highest point in the sky. Nature is at its peak and, like Beltane, this is an auspicious time to cast spells for love affairs, partnerships or marriage. This 'midsummer's night', we are invited to take control of our lives, empower ourselves and make a commitment to harvesting our personal goodness over the coming months.

Best for: this is the perfect season to collect the bountiful herbs and flowers that you can use as ingredients for spell work. Hang them to dry in a sunny spot and then store them in jars. Even if you're a solitary witch, perhaps join in a group event to appreciate the value of relationship and comradeship among fellow pagans. Maybe visit a sacred site where you can watch the solstice sunrise and soak in the atmosphere of this amazing moment when the sun 'stands still'. Midsummer's Eve is the perfect time to cast commitment spells for long-term love, self-love and for planning new goals for the future.

Lammas/Lughnasadh (1 August)

Lammas marks the midpoint between summer and autumn and heralds the first harvest of the year. It is a time for giving thanks for the summer's abundance and for the forthcoming autumn. Lughnasadh means 'festival of Lugh' and is named after the Celtic sun god. For many witches, this is the time when Lugh transfers his vitalising powers to the grain, and, once it has been harvested and baked into bread, he begins to descend to the darkness, ready to be reborn at Yule. This 'in-between' time of year is one of gratitude. It reveals that waiting for the approaching great harvest is rather like the in-between time when you have cast your spell and are waiting in anticipation for its manifestation.

Best for: spells that encourage speedier results for goals that seem to be slow to get moving. This is also a time to gather fruits, forage for nature's wild harvest in your local area and to place local produce on your altar to celebrate the coming of autumn. Use this day to plan and cast spells for new challenges or experiences in the months ahead. Be aware of how planning a goal is as enriching as the harvest or the actual manifestation of it. All it takes to work this magic is a little gratitude and the sowing of your initial 'seeds' with care and real dedication to your intention.

Autumn equinox (c. 21 September, northern hemisphere)

As the sun moves into Libra, represented by the Scales, there is a change of energy, as day and night are almost equal in length again. We start to find balance and harmony in our lives, ready for the darker days ahead. This is a time to be compassionate towards others and cast spells for equality and respect in all relationships. Wiccans celebrate the return of the Goddess, now a discerning crone, her wisdom at its height. The Druids honoured the 'god of the forest', leaving offerings of harvested herbs, cider or fruit wine under oak trees. Perhaps do the same to give thanks to both God and Goddess (masculine and feminine principles), fundamental to the balance of energy of the equinox.

Best for: this is a time to cast spells for personal growth, to take charge of your life, adapt to changing circumstances and for empowering relationships with good fortune. Gather fruits you recognise, like wayside blackberries, or go foraging for nature's wilder harvests. Avoid fungi, unless you have an expert alongside you. Collect fallen leaves and twigs of berries to decorate your altar, or press red maple leaves into your journal to use in spells later to add autumnal grounding to all your spell work.

Samhain (31 October)

Pronounced mostly 'sow-wen' (that's 'sow', as in a female pig), Samhain means 'summer's end', and, for most of us, this day is associated with Halloween. For some Celtic trad-itions, this was the start of their new year, as it marked the last day of the harvest year. It is said that this is a time when the boundary between the spiritual and mundane world is no longer defined and we can catch a glimpse into the numinous realm. It is a time to honour the past and our ancestors, and to set intentions for the coming Yule season. As the days grow darker and colder, and trees cover the earth with rotting leaves, the sun god begins to die away and the Goddess is at her greatest power, ready to give birth to the sun god at Yule and for a new cycle to begin.

Best for: cast spells around this time to invoke passion, mystery and more magic in your life and start manifesting serious ambitions and personal power. With the sun in Scorpio, review any deep-seated intentions you have for the future; calculate your options, prioritise your choices and perform rituals to align you to the power of any deities you have chosen to help you. This is the perfect time to call on spirits, fairies, your ancestors or any other spiritual entities you wish to help you with manifesting your goals.

Days of the Week

Each day of the week is associated with a deity. So in witch-craft, working on specific days enhances the effects of the spell in question, depending on the ruling god/goddess. For example, if you wanted to cast a spell to manifest more money, you might choose Venus' day (Friday). Named after her Norse equivalent, Freya, Venus rules not only love, but also money and material possessions.

Monday

The changeable moon rules Monday, so if you're seeking a change of direction, a new pathway or new opportunities, this is the day to do so, particularly during a waxing-moon phase (see Glossary, p. 283), which maximises the energy.

Tuesday

Named originally after the Roman god Mars, Tuesday is a day of impulse, action and motivational energy, and is also associated with leadership and courage. Spells cast on a Tuesday are favourable for initiation of ideas, intentions aligned to pioneering activity, determined goal setting and anything requiring strength of mind or physical courage.

Wednesday

We are bestowed with a logical mindset and a sharp, clever wit if we work with magic on this day, associated with the Greek god Hermes and the Roman god Mercury. Wednesday amplifies clarity, focus and forethought in all rituals and spells, so any short-term intentions that require clear thinking, communication or decision making are best cast on this day.

Thursday

Thursday is named after the Greek god Zeus and his counterpart Jupiter. Both represent abundance, prosperity and big ideas. Ruling Sagittarius, Jupiter helps us to seek out truth and self-knowledge or expand our horizons through travel, education and spiritual pursuits. This is the day to cast spells for wealth, plenty, travel or new projects.

Friday

Named after the Roman goddess Venus, as mentioned above, Friday is a day for love, social indulgences and even a little retail therapy. As Venus is the astrological planet of love, harmony, money and possessions, Friday is auspicious for casting spells connected to romance, love affairs, money, pleasure, creativity and investment in one's values and oneself.

Saturday

Saturn rules Saturday and is the god associated with responsibility, discipline and boundaries – as the rhyme goes, 'Saturday's child works hard for its living'. So this is the day for realising that you can be successful, as long as you work hard. Saturday is perfect for casting spells that are realistic, down to earth, pragmatic or for long-term projects that will stand the test of time.

Sunday

Ruled by the sun god, Sunday is very much associated with rest, family gatherings and giving thanks, due to its religious associations. In astrology the sun represents the centre of ourselves and what matters to us, so in witchcraft this is a day for manifesting spells to promote integrity and harmony in your home or lifestyle.

Whenever or wherever you cast your spells, you now have all the basic tools and witch's wisdom to get you started on your manifesting journey,

With all the knowledge you have so far gleaned, it would be a nice idea to show your commitment to your intentions by dedicating yourself to your new-found witchy self.

....

SELF-DEDICATION RITUAL

This ritual will reveal to the universe that you are being true to yourself. It's worth repeating it a few times a year (maybe on the major sabbats – see p. 130) to realign to this awareness.

You will need:
* A white tea light
* Flowers, herbs and petals
* Sandalwood incense or a few drops of essential oil
* A red tea light
* A bowl of leaves, nuts or fruit
* A length of coiled twine
* A glass of mineral water or cup of green tea (or wine, if you prefer)

1. On the evening of a waxing moon, light the white tea light for atmosphere.

2. Place the flowers and herbs on your table or altar and scatter petals over the top.

3. Fill the room with sandalwood fragrance, either with incense or by sprinkling the essential oil on to a favourite crystal.

4. Now place your symbols of the four elements as the four compass points on your table: to the north, the bowl of leaves, nuts or fruit; to the south, the red candle, unlit; to the east, the coiled twine; and to the west, the mineral water, green tea or wine.

5. Call in the four directional spirits by saying:

> Spirit of the north, come to affirm my gift of Earth.
> Spirit of the south, come to seal my gift of Fire.
> Spirit of the east, come to embellish my gift of Air.
> Spirit of the west, come to consecrate my gift of Water.

As you say each line, hold up the associated symbol to face that direction, and, when you have finished, replace it before picking up the next.

6. Now gaze into the flame of the white tea light for a few moments to find stillness. If you listen very carefully, you may hear the spirits whispering kindness to you, the gods delighting in your presence or the four elements sending you their blessings. Imagine you are now at one with all the universal powers, and they will always be there to help.

You have now initiated yourself into your practice and connected to your inner witch. It's time to move on to Part Two.

PART TWO

Manifestation Spells and Charms

The collection of spells and charms in the following chapters is based on traditional witchcraft lore, using incantations, symbols and ingredients that correspond to an intention, desire or goal. They are designed for a variety of intentions and will enable you to get to know how to work with charms and spells before you adapt or create your own (more of which on p. 263). I have prescribed ingredients in these spells, but you can also refer to the Correspondence List on p. 275 if you want to adapt these or be more creative with your spell work.

Every manifestation spell heralds a change, a fresh start, a new beginning. But for any new beginning, you have to let go of any baggage that might be holding you back, such as a toxic relationship, low self-esteem or negative thinking.

With this in mind, and having practised all the self-awareness rituals in Part One, you should, by now, be feeling more confident, determined and empowered. But there is still one thing you need to do to help you move on from the old you. And it's the best manifestation spell you can ever do: manifesting the new, vibrant, revitalised and motivated you.

....

MANIFESTING THE REAL YOU

Authentic champagne only comes from the Champagne region of France, and no drink can legally call itself champagne unless it originates from there. Similarly, you are the only 'unique you' on this planet. So to manifest the authentic you, enjoy indulging in this simple spell.

You will need:
* 9 stones
* A paper bag
* A small bottle of bubbly or other sparkling drink

1. On the evening of a waning moon, take your stones (these don't need to be special to you – you can collect them from the country-side, garden or beach; they are going to represent negative things in your past) and place them in the paper bag.

2. Take the bag outside, along with your chosen sparkling drink. Sit comfortably on the ground or a seat of your choice and gaze up at the evening sky.

3. Imagine yourself as one of the stars. Maybe focus on one that stands out for you, or one you have already identified – perhaps a planet with which you feel an affinity? This star shines brightly, radiant in its own place in the celestial canopy. It is, in fact, one of the privileged 'champagne' stars of the skies – unique, with its own qualities and powers.

4. Sit quietly for a minute or so while you reflect on this star and how it is actually a reflection of you – this special self.

5. Now take out a random stone from the bag. Reflect on what in particular it might represent – maybe a difficult relationship, a fear, a regret, a silly decision – then throw it away into the undergrowth. Take out another stone, reflect on something else in your past that it might represent and then throw it away. Repeat with the remaining stones. Each time a negative aspect of your life is thrown out, you are becoming more of your truly 'authentic' self.

6. When you have finished disposing of your unwanted baggage, screw up the paper bag in your hand as tightly as you can, vowing never to return to this old self.

7. Now raise your eyes to the sky and say out loud to the star: 'I now manifest who I am, the authentic me, the reawakened me, the one who will from now on be true to myself and my desires and follow them through. The past is gone, the present is a gift and the future is my destiny by choice.'

Just like a cork flying from a bottle of bubbly, you are now free, and can drink a toast to your inner witch and the manifestation of the real you.

Any time you feel any guilt, anger or hurt from the past resurfacing, or you have moments of doubt or vulnerability, visit your star in the sky and say, 'The most important decision I need to make now is to smile, manifest my future and dare to move on.'

As a reminder, before we get stuck in, the only 'must do' when practising witchcraft is to respect the magic, believe in it and do no harm to anyone, including yourself. Otherwise, there are no rules here – just guidance.

Now you have all the witchy wisdom you need – so let's start manifesting!

CHAPTER NINE

Manifesting Love and Romance

If you want the moon, do not hide from the night.
If you want a rose, do not run from the thorns.
If you want love, do not hide from yourself.
Rumi, thirteenth-century Persian poet

We all want love in our world – it's only natural; whether to feel *in* love or just embraced by the love of others. So this chapter is devoted to spells to manifest the kind of love you desire. There are spells for attracting new romance and for sustaining long-term commitment, as well as for letting go of heartbreak, banishing bad feelings of jealousy and getting over unrequited love. Here, you will also find charms to rekindle passion, encourage great physical chemistry and be ready to commit to the love of your life. But not everyone wants to commit for ever, so there are also spells based on free love; in other words, no strings, no promises – simply enjoying an open but caring relationship.

It's all very well reaching out to the universe and asking to manifest a new romance or lover into your life, but if you're not sending out the right signals, you're not going to get the right ones back. Self-love, as mentioned earlier (see p. 11), attracts love to you – self-assured people are attracted by self-assurance. We attract who we are. With this in mind, every time you perform a spell, ask yourself: who am I? For example, 'If I truly want romance, I must *be* or exude romance; I must work with my desire for romance and *be* romance myself.'

Note: many of the spells in this chapter draw on the attributes and powers of Venus/Aphrodite. This is because she is the most widely known goddess of love and it is her power through which most love manifests. However, if you prefer to substitute Aphrodite/Venus with a love deity of your own, please adapt the words or symbols accordingly.

EMPOWER YOURSELF WITH CHARISMA SPELL

Charisma means 'grace of the gods' and is associated with the three graces, or 'charites', of Greek mythology. Although individually they were known by many different names, Charis (also known as Aglaea) represented 'grace' itself, while Thalia represented 'blooming' and Euphrosyne 'joy'.

Venus/Aphrodite was, among other things, quite vain, and her charismatic presence ensured that most of the lovers she chose responded as she desired. We all have charisma, but some people and goddesses are more adept than others at casting this magic around them. They work their own spells, charming and beguiling everyone they meet.

All you need do is channel a little of Charis' grace and Venus' vanity, and with this spell you will be on the right track for persuading, seducing and generally shining your own charismatic light wherever you go.

You will need:

* A basket or bag filled with bunches of flowers, grasses, twigs and leaves – enough to scatter around you in a circle
* A clear quartz crystal

1. On a Friday (Venus' day) and preferably a sunny one (to also invite the light of the sun god), stand outside – somewhere in the country-side, if possible. Relax and find stillness.

2. When you feel ready, place your basket on the ground and hold the crystal high above your head with both hands.

3. Raise your face to the sky and say:
    > Charis and Venus are with me now,
    > To bring me charisma of that I vow.
    > By powers of nature and crystal charms,
    > I'm filled with spirit and loving arms.

4. Place the crystal next to your feet, take up your basket and scatter the contents all around you in a circle. As you do so, imagine you are spreading charisma wherever you go.

5. Pick up your crystal and step out of the circle.

'Grace' will naturally exude from you if you take the crystal with you wherever you go. If you ever experience a sense of insecurity or vulner-ability, hold the crystal close to your navel to re-ignite your charismatic spark.

LOVE JAR TO MANIFEST THE QUALITY OF ROMANCE

It's all very well bumping into the love of your life at work, socially or online, but romance is fickle and often elusive. So here's how to become a fabulous beacon to attract romance to you in the vast expanse of the universe.

You will need:
* A pink tea light
* A scrap of paper and a pen
* A glass jar with a lid or cork stopper
* A handful of dried basil leaves
* A handful of rose petals
* 2 rose quartz crystals
* A clear quartz crystal

1. On the evening of a full moon, sit down and light the tea light for atmosphere, and place your other ingredients before you.

2. On the piece of paper write a few words that sum up your intention, such as 'Bring romance to me' or, 'Attract romantic love into my life'. Be as clear and as concise as you can, and truly 'know' what you want before you write it down.

3. Repeat your intention aloud three times as you focus on the candle flame, then place the folded paper into the jar.

4. Add the basil, petals and crystals to jar, repeating your intention with each item.

5. Close the jar and say, 'Thank you, Aphrodite, for bringing romance to my life'.

6. Place the jar near a window to energise it with the full moon's power.

Leave your petition for at least one lunar cycle to encourage romantic love to enter your world.

....

YOUR BEWITCHMENT SACHET

Use this ancient recipe for a bewitchment sachet (believed to be a favourite concoction used by Madame de Montespan to seduce Louis XIV of France) to keep with you on any first date.

You will need:
* A red tea light
* A small organza sachet or pouch
* A small handful of lavender (dried or fresh flowers, crumbled)
* A few rose petals
* Patchouli oil
* A tiny rose quartz or rough ruby crystal
* A red ribbon

1. Light the tea light for atmosphere, then fill your sachet with the lavender, rose petals, a drop of patchouli oil and the crystal.

2. Tie the filled pouch with the red ribbon and, as you do so, say:

> This lavender's for wooing.
>
> This rose is for swooning.
>
> This crystal's for cocooning.
>
> This sachet's for tingling.
>
> This patchouli's for mingling.

3. Take the pouch/sachet with you in your bag or pocket and see the sparkle manifest in your date's eyes.

If you are charmed, too, keep the sachet under your pillow to encourage a further date. If not, simply remove the crystal after your date and wash it in spring water, then sprinkle the rest of the ingredients into the nearest rubbish bin and the spell will be un-cast.

Apples in Magic

Apples have long been associated with love and also the problems it can cause. In Greek mythology, Eris (the goddess of discord), furious that she hadn't been invited to a wedding feast, threw a golden apple among the guests, inscribed 'to the fairest'. Paris, the prince of Troy, was given the job of deciding the winner among the squabbling goddesses. He chose Aphrodite, who bribed him by offering him as his consort the most beautiful woman in the world – Helen of Sparta. In so doing, she set off the Trojan War.

ARE THEY WORTHY OF YOU?

This mediaeval spell is less about strife and more about guaranteeing a good love life. To ensure you have attracted a trustworthy mate, and not a player, catfish or otherwise unworthy admirer, this apple spell will manifest the truth.

You will need:
* An apple
* Lemon or wild orange essential oil

1. On the evening of a waxing moon, cut the apple in half widthwise, and lay each half on your table.

2. Focus on the five-star (pentagram) formation of the pips in one half of the apple and, as you do so, ask the universe: 'Is this person true and trustworthy?'

3. Repeat the question five times, touching one of the pips each time.

4. Now release one drop of oil on to the pips of the half you were touching, and gently press the two halves together and leave on the table overnight.

In the morning, if the oil has not been absorbed, it is a sign that this person is not to be trusted. If the apple has absorbed the oil, however, you can go ahead and get to know them better.

DIVINING WITH APPLES

Bobbing for apples is a well-known party game played at Halloween. It was originally a traditional pastime associated with the celebration of Samhain, when apples were key produce at harvest time. In the Samhain game, an apple was scratched with the name of an intended lover. Each suitor had three chances to grab the apple with their teeth. If they hadn't managed to hold on to it after three tries, the relationship was doomed to failure, according to superstition.

Here's a fun way to determine if it's worth proceeding with a relationship if you're looking for something more permanent than just a fling.

You will need:
* A clear quartz crystal
* A large, fairly deep bowl filled with spring water (enough for the apples to float)
* 2 red apples

1. Place the crystal in the bottom of the bowl, and then float the two apples on top.

2. Gaze into the water at the crystal and focus on the relationship in question.

3. Cross your hands behind your back and when you feel ready, ask out loud: 'Is this relationship long-term?'

4. Put your lips to the first apple and try to grab it with your teeth. If you succeed in three tries and can keep it between your teeth for five seconds before dropping it on the table, the answer to your question is yes.

5. Next, ask, 'Is it worth continuing this relationship?'

6. Put your lips to the second apple. If you manage to grab it within three attempts, the answer is yes.

If you have a negative result with either question, it's most likely this is not the best relationship for you.

....

SUMMER SOLSTICE CHARM FOR COMMITMENT

As the sun moves into 0° Cancer on 21 June (although the exact moment in time can vary depending on the year), it marks the astronomical and astrological beginning of summer. We often call this Midsummer's Eve but, whether you feel it as the debut of summer or the middle, the most important thing for our purposes is that the sun is now at a moment of 'solstice' or 'standing still'. This has traditionally been a sacred time for making the most of the longest hours of daylight before the turn of the wheel rotates towards winter.

Be sure to profit from the energy of this day – it's the perfect chance to seal and manifest a long-term commitment. You can either do this spell with your partner, if their intention is as true and committed as yours, or you can do it alone (as long as you have utter faith that your intended is on the same page as you).

You will need:
* 9 roses (any colour you like)
* 9 stones or pebbles found in the garden, beach or countryside (make sure you have permission to remove them)
* 9 leaves (any that you choose)
* 9 small shells
* A red apple
* A pin or needle
* A handful of sunflower seeds, as needed

1. Preferably outside, on the evening before the day of the solstice, make a large circle with the nine roses.

2. Working inwards, make another circle of stones, then one of leaves, then, finally, the innermost one of shells.

3. Carve your initials on the side of the apple with the pin or needle, with your partner's initials entwined in yours. Place the apple inside the innermost circle.

4. Sit before your circle of love, and say:
> With roses nine I give my love.
> With pebbles nine they/he/she give(s) to me.
> With shells of nine we share our love.
> With leaves of nine forever 'we'.
> This thirty-six return to nine,
> And from this day our pledge will be.

5. Leave your sacred circle overnight.

6. On the morning of the solstice, cut the apple in half and place nine seeds in a safe, box or jar to seal your intention for long-term love (if there are more than nine seeds, throw the others away; if there are fewer, make up the number with some sunflower seeds).

7. Dismantle your sacred circle to end the spell.

Watch how your commitment flourishes, and, if you ever need reassurance of your partner's, take the seeds from your box and hold them in your hand for two minutes – you will realise that their love is here to stay.

Romance and Commitment Spells

There are many other kinds of spells to attract and nurture romance, so why not try some of these?

....

WHISPER WORDS OF LOVE SPELL

If you already know someone with whom you feel a connection and want to take it a little further – whether a second date, a first kiss or more – this spell will encourage exactly that. It will only work if the intended admirer already has a similar intention towards you, however (don't forget – we can't use witchery to control or manipulate other people's feelings).

You will need:
*   A piece of paper and a pen
*   A piece of citrine

1. Write your intention on the piece of paper. For example, 'X is asking me for a second date'. (Write it as an active, present-tense statement, as if it is actually happening, as opposed to, 'I really hope X might call me'.)

2. Below your intention, draw a sketch of an ear. It doesn't have to be accurate or artistically brilliant – just an outline of the shape of an ear.

3. Place the citrine below your sketch.

4. Close your eyes and, when you feel centred and still, open them again and take up the piece of citrine. Holding it close to your third-eye chakra (see p. 283), say:

   > With third eye now I find my voice
   > To whisper out my words of choice,
   > To tell this one that I'm for you,
   > And they will hear my words ring true.

5. Hold the citrine to your lips and whisper your intention, as if to the crystal.

6. Repeat your intention nine times.

7. End by placing the citrine in the middle of your drawing and leave overnight.

If your message was clear and strong and your intended was listening to your whispers, they will respond in the way you desire.

STIR LOVE BETWEEN YOU

So you've got past the first few dates, and you are now officially dating. But do you want this to go a little further? Do you want more than just physical fun, romance and the anticipation of the next date? Do you, deep down, really want a lot more?

As before, you can't force things by using this spell. It only works on the basis that love will grow if it's a mutual thing.

You will need:
* 2 red tea lights
* A dark red (or other dark-coloured) bowl, filled with water
* 2 drops of patchouli essential oil
* A long-stemmed red rose, the stem bound with red ribbon

1. On a full-moon evening, light the tea lights and place one either side of the bowl of water.

2. Drop the oil into the water. (You will see the water and oil separate, representing you and your intended.)

3. When you are ready and feel centred, take up the rose at the flower end, and gently start to swirl the ribbon-bound stem around in the water in a clockwise direction. Imagine, as you gaze into the dark water, that you are stirring love between the two of you; imagine, as you stir, that hearts grow kinder, passion blossoms, love flows between you, healing, giving and receiving.

4. Lift the stem from the bowl and, as the water continues to swirl around, drop in one rose petal and say:

> I stir happiness into our hearts.
> I stir loyalty into our souls.
> I stir belief into our love.
> I stir truth into our words.
> I stir love between us.

5. Repeat with nine more petals (and keep stirring, so the water continues to swirl around).

6. Let the water come to a stop of its own accord and blow out your candles.

If love has been stirred equally between you, your partner will soon show it in the way they act, speak to and cherish you.

....

MUTUAL-BINDING SPELL

As mentioned earlier, the Greek moon goddess, Selene, was so in love with the mortal shepherd Endymion that she put him into an eternal sleep, so she could visit him each night and make love to him. It's now time to draw down the power of the lunar goddess, to bring you her blessing and tie a love knot between you and your partner.

If you and your partner have already started looking towards a more committed relationship, this mutual-binding spell will seal that intention and promote greater ties between you. However, you need to do this together and be sure of your loyal intentions – because although we can encourage others to feel some kind of mutual bond, we cannot force them to feel bound to us.

You will need:
* A bowl of spring water
* 2 x 90cm lengths of red ribbon or cord
* 2 roses
* 2 rose quartz crystals

1. With your partner, on the evening of a full moon, take all your ingredients outside and sit cross-legged, facing one another.

2. Place the bowl between you, and beside it the ribbons, flowers and crystals.

3. Each of you place a crystal in the bowl, and say together, 'Thank you, Goddess, for blessing our future love.'

4. Now take up a ribbon each, and wind it around and around your other wrist, tucking the end into the binding to secure it.

5. Hold your hands out, palms and wrists touching, so the ribbons touch, too, then say:
     By the light of the moon and her power to bind,
     We perform this magic for both to unwind.

6. Now each of you take up a rose (in your ribbon-bound hands) and hand it into the other's unbound hand. Place your roses down beside you.

7. Now each of you take a crystal from the water (with your unbound hands) and hold and touch the two crystals to each other for about

ten seconds, as you both say:

> With this crystal in waters calm
> We call on the moon to bring her charm.

This will draw down the power of the moon.

8. Place the crystals beside the roses, unbind your wrists, then swap crystals, roses and ribbons.

Keep each other's crystals, roses and ribbons beneath your bed for one lunar cycle to manifest your mutual commitment to long-term love.

....

BELTANE SPELL TO PROMOTE JOY AND SEXUAL HARMONY

Beltane is a time for fertility, growth, anticipatory romances, pledges and whispers, promises and physical union. Hand-fasting was (and has recently become again) a popular custom, whereby young couples join their hands and commit themselves 'for a year and a day, at least'.

Be actively seductive once you have performed this spell to ensure the magic works to manifest sexual harmony, enhance physical joy and the chemistry between you and your partner or an admirer. This means that you have to literally engage in some form of seductive pleasure, rather than just imagine it will happen by chance.

You will need:
* A red tea light
* A mirror
* A phial or small glass bottle with a lid
* 3 drops of patchouli oil

* 3 drops of rose essential oil
* 3 drops of oud or sandalwood essential oil
* A small rough ruby

1. On the evening before Beltane (so on 30 April), light your candle, and sit calmly before your mirror and gaze at yourself.

2. For a few minutes, imagine or visualise your intended lover or partner in the mirror before you, their eyes burning into yours with fierce desire, as passionate and strong as the candle flame.

3. Open the phial and release the oils into it, then close the lid and mix them together by shaking gently. As you do so, say:

   As above so below,
   My love for you just grows and grows.
   Our passion greater than a flame
   Unites our bodies, wild, untamed.

4. Place the phial down, then take up the rough ruby and hold it just below your navel (the centre of your sexual energy flow) for two minutes. As you hold it there, focus on the thought of making love to your partner or chosen lover and imagine the waves of joy flowing through you.

5. Let go of the image, blow out the candle and leave the ruby before the mirror, next to the phial, until the morning.

6. On the morning of Beltane, as early as you can, take your phial outside, run your hand through the grass or weeds and scoop some morning dew (the magical essence of the goddess of the dawn, Eos) into the phial. If you can't find any, simply write the word 'dew' on a tiny scrap of paper and drop that in instead.

165

7. Back at your table or altar, relight the candle.

8. Open the phial and dab a tiny spot of the mixture on the back of each of your wrists, and say:

> Dressed with love and Beltane's power,
> We fall together not apart.
> In rich desire we weave our spell,
> For perfumed dew and sexual art.

9. During the day, find joy in as many things as you can in nature, even seeing a bird fly or hearing a bee buzz to fire your intention for sexual joy to the universe.

When you do meet up with your partner, the harmonious Beltane magic will begin!

Spells for Letting Go and Breaking Free

Many of us don't want to enter into a committed relationship. Some of us prefer to remain single, have an open relationship or just not commit yet. For whatever reason, making this choice means you have to make it very clear to the outside world, or possible relationship partners, that this is your intention. Otherwise, others out there may well make assumptions based on their own values about what a relationship means to them.

A SPELL TO ENCOURAGE AN
UNCOMMITTED RELATIONSHIP

This spell will invisibly emit the right signals and attract those who have the same values as you. (Of course, it's not foolproof, but at least you will be clarifying to the universe what you want to manifest, and therefore you're more likely to get a response from those who are in tune with you.)

You will need:
* A glass bowl filled with spring water
* A clear quartz crystal
* A piece of red carnelian

1. On the evening of a waxing moon, place the bowl of water on your altar or table, and put the two crystals, side by side, in the bottom of the bowl.

2. Focus on the crystals for a few moments and, as you do so, think about the kind of relationship you would like: free of commitment, free of conditions, free and easy. Imagine yourself having no ties, being single, perhaps dating as and when you desire. If this image builds into something powerful in your mind, continue with the spell. However, if you have any doubts and think, Oh, what if I meet 'the one'? maybe you need to reflect on your true values and whether you are sure of your desire for this type of relating.

3. If you are sure, remove the two crystals (now they have been purified) and hold them against your navel, as you say:
    With red carnelian, I find my way,

167

Unique, uncluttered as free as day.
With crystal clear, my heart is set
To take this road alone as yet.

4. Keep the clear quartz crystal under your pillow for one lunar cycle and carry the red carnelian with you wherever you go.

Those who share your desire for singledom and a free spirit will be attracted to you, to create the kind of relationship you thrive on.

....

LETTING OTHERS GO, AND FREEDOM FROM UNWANTED ATTENTION

Love isn't just about drawing people to us – it's also about letting others leave us, and loving them from afar, however painful it is to let go. Sometimes it's also about putting up boundaries or making it clear that you do not actually feel a connection. Without hurting someone, you may have to gently divert their attention elsewhere. That, in itself, is giving out a different kind of love, so that others may continue to discover love elsewhere. To either manifest freedom from unwanted attention or open your arms and let someone go and love them from afar, this spell will work within one lunar cycle, if you truly believe in the magic.

You will need:
* A piece of black obsidian
* A piece of malachite
* 5 basil leaves
* A hand mirror

1. On the evening of a waning moon, place the two stones on the table side by side, and surround them with a five-pointed star of basil leaves.

2. Take up the mirror and hold it with the reflected surface pointing away from you, towards the two stones, and say, 'This mirror reflects unwanted energy and protects my world. It will ensure that all the intentions you/I have will align with someone who can share your love. So mote it be' (meaning 'So may it be').

3. Pick up the stones and place the mirror face down in the centre of the basil leaves.

4. Place the malachite on top of the mirror.

5. Holding the black obsidian, if you are seeking freedom from unwanted attention, say, 'Dear universe, please cut all energy, physical, psychic, emotional and spiritual between me and [their name] and let all their desire for me end, from this day and forever more.' (If you are intending to let someone go, but love them from afar, say: 'Dear universe, please let [their name] be happy and allow me to let them go, but still love them from afar, from this day and forever more.')

6. Place the black obsidian on top of the mirror, beside the malachite.

7. Leave overnight, and in the morning take up the basil leaves and bury them in the garden or somewhere in the countryside where they cannot be found.

By the next waning moon, your unwanted interest will have found someone new or you will feel able to let go of someone, and still love them from afar.

....

BREAK-AN-INFATUATION SPELL

So you fell for their eyes, the way they look, their laughter, their brain-power? You may have even had a one-night stand, but it didn't mean anything to them. Yet you still can't stop looking out for them, hoping they'll notice you. Frankly, you know you're infatuated – you can't stop thinking about them – but maybe you're also beginning to realise this is one crush you can do without. Maybe they are already spoken for or simply have no interest in taking things any further . . .

Use this unbinding spell to help release you from your infatuation without causing the other person any harm. This is more successful if performed during a waning- or dark-of-the-moon phase.

You will need:
* 3 x 90cm lengths of black ribbon
* A small piece of paper and a pen
* Scissors

1. Make a plait with the three ribbons, knotting it off at both ends.

2. Coil the plait around the wrist of your writing hand, then tuck the end in to keep it in place.

3. With your bound wrist, take your piece of paper and write the name of the one in question over and over again – it can be scribbled big or small, perhaps in red ink, and the bolder, the better. Each time you scrawl their name, repeat over and over again in your mind: please release me from this infatuation.

4. When you have covered the page, unwind your plaited ribbon from your wrist, place it in the centre of the paper, and say out loud: 'Free me now from this darkness, free me now from this bind, as I cut through the infatuation, so mote it be.'

5. With your scissors, cut the ribbons up into pieces (as small as you like – and please take care), until they are in shreds. Keep repeating the line in step 4, as you cut and snip.

6. When you have finished cutting, you may already feel a sigh of relief, as the unbinding releases you from your crush.

7. Finish by crossing out all the writing on your paper, then wrap the paper around the ribbon shreds and throw it all into a rubbish bin.

You will no longer be bound by this infatuation. If you still feel you are, repeat the spell until you are released.

....

RITUAL TO SOOTHE AND CURE A BROKEN HEART

Breaking up is one of the hardest things we can ever do in a love relationship. Most of us know only too well the pain of a broken heart, whether it's the result of a mutual agreement, being dumped after just a date or two or, worse, a betrayal in what appeared to be a cosy, long-term relationship.

As devastating as it is, denying the pain isn't the answer. You must allow your feelings to come through, but not overcome you. You may never 'get over' this relationship, or your feelings of loss, anger, sadness or despair, but you will get through it with self-respect, and mostly with the help of new intentions for yourself.

But a broken heart is still a broken heart, so to help mend it – just enough to free yourself from the attachment, so you can move on – perform this spell, preferably during a waning- or dark-of-the-moon phase. The spell won't harm your ex, but it will take the 's' out of feeling 'cursed' to help you on your way to feeling 'cured'.

You will need:
* A pin or needle
* 2 tapered black candles
* A piece of black obsidian
* A piece of citrine

1. With the pin, scratch your initials on one candle, and your ex's on the other.

2. Light both candles safely, and watch them burn down for a while, focusing on your intention to start afresh (you can even write it down).

3. Hold the black obsidian in your palms and say, 'With this stone, I am freed of negativity and blame. I am protected and safe from the darkness.'

4. Place the stone on your altar or table, and then pick up the citrine and say, 'With this stone I am filled with light, new beginnings and joy is mine again.'

5. Gaze into the flame of your ex's candle for a moment, then say: 'With love and respect, I send you only goodness for your future. I now release my attachment to you.'

6. Blow out the candle.

7. Now gaze at your own candle, and say, 'This black candle will soon burn out, and, when it does so, all dark negativity and unfulfilled hopes, dreams and bad feelings for myself will be gone.'

8. Blow out the candle.

9. Relight the candles every evening, repeat the above, then blow them out.

Continue to repeat the above for as many days as it takes for both candles to burn right down (always stay with them when they're alight). Once they have finally burned out, you will begin to be able to move on, with new intentions for your personal happiness.

....

MOVING-ON SPELL TO HELP RESTORE SELF-ESTEEM

Note: this spell is not a remedy for any mental-health issue that requires professional attention.

Once you've let go of past baggage, however painful that can seem, you need to manifest some renewed self-esteem and give yourself a sense that you deserve love, just by virtue of being on this planet.

But you know something? In our modern, witchy world, we are always talking about ways to overcome feelings of pain, bitterness, regret and so on, often forgetting an innate human need to experience our feelings – to express love and hate in a positive way, to ride with our emotions, whether to soar high as a summer swallow or plummet into a sea of misery. Yes, we are human, but the ancient 'wildness' in us needs to be liberated now and then.

Here's a spell for expressing anger, then letting it go and allowing it to be replaced by a sense of self-worth and acceptance.

You will need:
* A rose with thorns
* An apple or pear

1. On the evening of a waning moon, go outside with your rose and fruit, and sit somewhere quiet.

2. Reflect on the pain that you feel, whether from rejection, betrayal or loss – whatever it is that has made you bleak and feeling unloved or unworthy. If you weep, that's ok – don't hold it in; if you start feeling anger, let it well up, shout and swear a bit or pummel the ground, if it makes you feel better.

3. Once you have let go a little, take a few deep breaths and pick up the rose carefully in one hand.

4. Press your other hand against the rose's stem gently, until you feel the thorns start to dig into your skin just a tiny bit (you don't have to be a masochist to perform this spell!). It may hurt a bit, a lot or maybe not at all.

5. Now smell the rose. What does it smell like? Sweet, or of nothing much?

6. Now bite into the apple or pear. Does it taste good, bad or just of nothing?

174

7. Now take both the rose and the fruit and bury them in the ground (or throw them in a green-waste bin) and, as you do so, realise you are 'burying' the bad taste, the sharp pain, the sweet memories, even the tasty ones. You are burying all of it – not just the bad, but all the good that was there, too – so that you are cleansed, free of the past and finally putting it to rest.

By the next full moon, you will feel your self-esteem returning. It will restore you to a belief in yourself and in the world around you – the world that cares for you and is filled with wondrous things. If only you dare look beyond the thorns of the rose or the sweet taste of the fruit, you'll soon be able to say, 'It seems I loved you once, but I love myself a thousand times more.'

The collection of spells in this chapter has covered *most* desires of the heart, from romance to long-term commitment. For spells that deal with the love between family and friends, move on to the next chapter.

CHAPTER TEN

Manifesting a Happy Family, Friends and Home

*That is part of the beauty of all literature. You discover
that your longings are universal longings, that you're
not lonely and isolated from anyone. You belong.*
F. Scott Fitzgerald, American novelist

I f you are lucky enough to be 'friends' with your family,
rather than just tolerating one another, you're off to a good
start. But even the most accepting, understanding and
caring clan can become tainted by too much familiarity. So
to keep the peace, encourage a sense of belonging and
harmony in the home, while enabling you to stay true to
your own individuality, this chapter is devoted to manifesting good relationships among families – and friends, too.

....

GRID FOR GENERAL HARMONY IN THE HOME

Hestia, the Greek goddess of the home, hearth and altar, was associated with fire, garnets and candle flames, so this spell calls on her to encourage better relating for a harmonious home.

You can set up the grid on your altar or special table space, or you can leave it on a ledge or surface where other family members won't be able to disturb it.

You will need:
* A red tea light
* 5 small pieces of citrine
* 5 small pieces of black tourmaline
* 5 small pieces of garnet
* A piece of clear quartz crystal for each family member

1. Carefully light the candle to welcome Hestia to your home.

2. Lay the citrine pieces out in the shape of a pentagram, with the top pointing due north. (You may need a compass, unless you already know the directions in your home.)

3. Lay a black tourmaline piece in between each citrine and the garnets in a small circle in the centre of your pentagram.

4. Hold the clear quartz pieces in your hands over the pentagram, and say, 'From this day, the hearth will warm us, the flame of love will come and keep us from harm. We'll share that love and care for one another. Thank you, Hestia, for all you do.'

5. Repeat the above affirmation as many times as there are people in your family.

6. Place the quartz pieces in the centre of the circle and, for a few moments, focus on the happy home you seek, each member of your family and how you live in harmony.

7. When you feel you are ready, blow out the candle and leave the room.

Hestia's empowering crystals will continue to disperse harmony throughout your home over the coming weeks.

. . . .

PEACEMAKER POUCH

We all want to be happy in the home, but there will always be rifts, disagreements, mood changes and conflicting needs. And after a dispute, there may be lingering tensions in the air – a disgruntled energy, carrying toxic anger, resentment, negativity and so on.

To clear this energy, and to restore the gentle hearts of all family members, create a peacemaker pouch. Soon, you'll be happy in each other's company again.

You will need:
* A white tea light
* 2 yellow tea lights
* 3 beech leaves
* 3 oak leaves

* A small organza sachet/pouch
* A piece of amethyst

1. Cast a magic circle of protection around you and your ingredients to ensure that all the negative energy of others who live with you is banished from your space (see p. 120).

2. On your altar or table, light the white tea light, then place the two yellow ones either side of it and light them, too.

3. Put the beech and oak leaves in the organza pouch, followed by the amethyst.

4. Close the sachet, shake it gently and say three times, 'Spirits of the sky, the planets and the Earth, revive peace in this home between all family members, and attract goodwill to us. I give thanks to the universe for manifesting calm and harmony.'

5. Now blow out all three candles to fire your intention to the universe.

Hide the sachet somewhere in the home, not far from the main entrance, so that every time you or family members enter or leave you will all be instilled with kindness and goodwill.

....

PROTECTION FROM PSYCHIC NEGATIVITY

The spirits of the home (known as the 'lares' and 'penates' in Roman folklore) are ever-present invisibles, and can be called upon to help protect you against any negative energy entering your home. This kind of psychic pollution is often carried unintentionally by guests and strangers alike; whether it's the plumber or your best friend's new partner, they may have no intention of disrupting your peaceful, harmonious home, but they can leave traces of their own auras, rife with personal problems and difficulties. Here's how to protect your home.

You will need:
* A small round wooden or glass bowl
* 5 dried basil leaves
* 3 pieces of black tourmaline
* 3 drops of lavender essential oil

1. Line the bottom of the bowl with the basil leaves and place the black tourmaline pieces on top.

2. Dress the crystals with the lavender essential oil, and say, 'Thank you, spirits of the home, for protecting us from outside negativity'.

3. Leave the bowl discreetly near your main entrance and top up the oil once a week (always at the same time that you set up the initial spell).

This spell will help you to maintain a good connection to the lares and penates of your household so that, when the person in question leaves your home, any psychic dust goes with them, and you and your family will be protected from intrusive negative energy.

FAMILY TREE OF LIFE

The tree of life is a motif that features in many mythologies worldwide. For example, it appears as an icon of mystical Jewish kabbalah – the pathway to spiritual enlightenment; it is well known as Yggdrasil, or the world tree of Norse mythology; and there is the divine tree, Kalpavriksha, of Hindu, Buddhist and Jain cosmology, which, according to tradition, grants your every wish when placated with offerings.

To improve relations between siblings, parents, children and other family members, create a family tree of life, going back as many generations as you can to discover your family history and make a connection with any favoured ancestors you can call on to help you when you need their spiritual wisdom.

Perform this spell around either the harvesting celebrations of Lammas (1 August) or Samhain (31 October).

You will need:
* A slender branching stem from a tree or shrub that you find graceful and pleasing and would be happy to have in your home (preferably one that's fallen, but, if you need to prune a tree or bush for any reason, respectfully tell the tree what you are doing and why, and then thank them)
* A large vase
* Scraps of paper to write on, and/or images/photos of your family
* A pen/paper/paint
* A hole punch
* Gold ribbons

1. Purify your branch by removing all its leaves if it has any (you can dry them and keep them pressed or in a jar for future spells), then let it dry out in a sunny place for at least three days.

2. Arrange the branch in your vase, then choose the west corner of your home to maximise harmonious energy – somewhere you can stand the vase without it getting knocked over.

3. On the scraps of paper draw or paint images of all the family. Or you can just write their names or add photos.

4. Using your hole punch, make holes in the images and thread through the gold ribbon or twine.

5. Hang the images on your branches. Perhaps place the oldest or most important member at the top, if you feel this is relevant to your family. It's up to you to decide who goes where on this, your tree of life.

6. When you have finished, give thanks to your family and your ancestors for bringing harmony to the home by every full moon, touching each of the family 'leaves' in turn and repeating your gratitude.

The presence of this family tree in your home will maximise positive attitudes and behaviour from everyone in your family, helping to generate unconditional love, so that you will be more accepting of each other's differences of opinion or values.

KEEP HAPPINESS SAFE

It's all very well enhancing or manifesting harmony in the home, but you need to make sure it's a happy one, too. Do this simple spell every sabbat (see p. 130) to ensure your home is filled with love all year round.

You will need:
* Basil leaves (fresh or dried) – as many as required for the steps below
* Frankincense oil

1. Consecrate the basil leaves by releasing a drop of frankincense oil on to each one.

2. Place one leaf over each window and doorway in your home, and one under your doormat and any opening that leads to a cellar, garage, outbuilding, utility space, loft and so on.

3. Say aloud: 'This day, I bless my home and fill it with love all year round.'

Renew the leaves every sabbat, and your home will remain filled with happiness.

SPELL FOR MOVING HOME

Moving home can be a joyful experience, a new adventure, an escape, a way out of a difficult relationship or it can be filled with sadness, nostalgia for what was and what you may be leaving behind. It can be a welcome change, but also an unwelcome experience.

As soon as you have the key to your new place – even if you haven't moved your possessions in yet – do the following three practices to manifest a harmonious atmosphere and clear the home of any negativity from past occupants.

Clearing psychic energy

Light a sage smudge stick, so it's smoking. Take a slow walk around your new home, waving it in every corner, every cupboard, every angle, every window, above, beneath and around any furniture, if there is any left in the place. Carry it up staircases, down into cellars, covering every inch of your new abode – also, outside in the garden, if there is one, in sheds, garages and along terraces and entranceways and paths. Just everywhere. As you go around, say aloud, 'Begone old spirits, begone past occupants, begone geopathic stress, begone from here.' Repeat this over and over again, until you have finished your tour.

Blow out or extinguish your smudge stick and move on to the next practice.

Layout of crystals for home protection

Black tourmaline is the ultimate protection stone against negative energy, while black obsidian blocks geopathic stress and counters psychic attack. Selenite's pure energy vibration allows a constant positive energy flow to circulate your home.

You will need:
* A piece of black obsidian
* A piece of selenite
* A piece of black tourmaline

1. Place the black obsidian by your main entrance.

2. Leave the selenite and the black tourmaline in the room or space where you will sleep.

Leave the stones in place for at least two lunar cycles, and, every evening of a waning moon, gently cleanse the obsidian in spring water (it soaks up negativity like a sponge) and return it to its place of guardianship by the door.

The heart-of-the home stone
Lastly, you need to find a 'heart-of-the-home' stone. This will be a symbol of your dedicated new life in this home. Even if you are not happy about moving here, for whatever reason, this stone will encourage a positive sense of belonging.

Regardless of when you move into your home, this spell needs activating during a waxing moon to empower your stone with lunar positivity.

Take a walk in the countryside and, on your wanderings, look out for a stone that 'speaks' to you. It can be a pebble, a small rock, a tiny smooth stone on a beach or something you spot in your local habitat. You will know it when you see it, because in a way the stone is finding you.

Take it home, cleanse it in spring water, let it dry off, then place it in the heart of your home. This can be the place where you work or sit most of the time, by your bed if you prefer, or literally at the centre of your home according to its layout. When you place it, say, 'Thank you, stone, for finding me and knowing you will protect me and bring happiness and joy to this home.'

If and when you move out of this home, don't take the heart stone with you. Bury it in a secret place or near where you found it, to release it from the energy it has absorbed from your old abode.

....

THE 'GENIUS'-IN-A-BOTTLE SPELL

Every household in ancient Greek and Roman life respected and worshipped their family spirits who were welcome guardians in the home. These included the Roman genii who were protectors of specific places, individuals, plants or even a soil or vegetable patch in a garden. With your 'genius' in a bottle, you too can feel protected against any unwelcome energy around your home.

You will need:
* 3 small pieces of black tourmaline
* 1 teaspoon ground cinnamon or a stick of cinnamon
* 1 teaspoon black pepper
* 1 teaspoon sea salt
* A small screw-top bottle with lid
* A scrap of paper and a pen
* An orange tea light

1. Put the black tourmaline, cinnamon, black pepper and sea salt in your bottle.

2. Draw a circle on your scrap of paper and write your name and address on it, too. Put the paper in the bottle, put the lid on and place the bottle on your altar.

3. Light the orange candle beside the bottle, and say, 'The genius in this bottle will protect my home and all within it from negativity. So mote it be.'

4. Focus on the flame for a few minutes (you may even glimpse the genius dancing in your bottle, out of the corner of your eye!).

5. When you feel stilled and ready, blow out the candle and place the bottle near your front door in a discreet place.

Your genius is now ready to keep you protected.

....

LEAVING – HOME – FOR – GOOD TEA CEREMONY

If you're leaving home – whether you're feeling excited, nostalgic, wishing you could stay or wondering if you're doing the right thing – this simple spell will free you from any doubt or fear, and give you a sense of purpose for moving on.

You will need:
* A white tea light
* A pen and paper
* A handful of chamomile tea leaves
* A teapot and boiling water

1. Light the candle and draw a large circle on your piece of paper to represent you.

2. Fill the circle with words that describe your feelings, such as 'sad', 'regret', 'excitement', 'relief' and so on.

3. When you've covered the inside of the circle with words, scatter the tea leaves over the paper and, as you do so, say, 'I affirm that I am leaving this home, and wherever I go, I will no longer look back, but move on with gratitude.'

4. Use the paper to funnel the leaves into the teapot, along with the paper, and make an infusion by pouring boiling water over them.

5. Let it steep for a few minutes before sipping your tea.

As you drink, know that your tea ceremony is giving you positivity for leaving your home and moving on.

....

ATTRACTING A KINDRED SPIRIT

When we talk of kindred spirits, we usually mean people who share the same values, dreams, goals and intentions as us.

You feel an immediate affinity with a kindred spirit, as if you've known them for ever, or, some may say, in another life. You feel comfortable and happy to be yourself around this person who reflects your own nature. But how do you attract a kindred spirit to you?

First, of course, you need to be in the right place at the right time – perhaps via focusing on your true passions, values and joys in life, so you're more likely to 'bump into' them. But to help you on your way, perform this spell during a waxing- moon phase.

You will need:
* 2 x 90cm lengths of blue ribbon (for affinity)
* 2 x 90cm lengths of red ribbon (for spirit)
* 2 x 90cm lengths of gold ribbon (for joy)
* A ball of string

1. Take one ribbon of each colour, knot the ends together, braid the ribbons, then knot off the other end. Repeat with the other three ribbons so you have two braids.

2. Place your braids vertically side by side on your altar or table and surround them by winding the ball of string around them in an anti-clockwise direction to make a circle.

3. Cut the string from the ball and then say:
   > These ribbons show my spirit's true
   > To reach out far and come to you.
   > With blue we'll stir a kinship best,
   > And red for mutual passion's jest,
   > Then gold attracts our happy days,
   > And with this string we'll tie our ways.

4. Take up the string and knot one end around the middle of one braid and the other end around the middle of the second braid. Then drape the string over a mirror, doorway or window, so that the braids hang down.

Your twin braids will encourage a new kindred spirit to enter your life.

MAKING-UP SPELL

Sometimes even the best of pals fall out, and, whether trivial or serious, you can make up or repair any rift by calling on the Greek goddess Artemis, associated with the waxing crescent moon, and fresh starts and renewal. With the added power of amber in this spell (not a crystal as such, but fossilised tree resin), which removes toxic waste from relationships, you can rebuild your friendship and get back to being friends again.

Do this spell during a waxing moon.

You will need:
* A yellow tea light
* A piece of amber
* 2 drops of wild orange essential oil
* A handful of yellow rose petals

1. Light the candle and place it somewhere well away from wherever you are doing the next part of the spell.

2. Place the amber on your altar or table, drop the wild orange essential oil on to the amber, and then scatter the rose petals randomly across the crystal.

3. The petal that falls furthest away from you represents your pal, while the closest one represents you.

4. Take these two petals and put one on top of the other (it doesn't matter which way round).

5. Place the amber on top of the petals and say, 'I affirm to Artemis that from now on, this friendship bond will be repaired, any wounds healed and our relationship blessed.'

6. Repeat twice more, and then blow out the candle, as if blowing a kiss to your friend to seal your intention.

7. Get in touch with your friend before the next full moon and arrange to meet up. Take the amber with you, offer it to them as a reconciliation gift.

The crystal will soak up and disperse any negativity, so that the two of you can restart your relationship.

....

DISCOVER NEW FRIENDS

At certain times, you may need to seek out new pals, whether due to educational or job changes, moving home and so on. Or you may simply desire to expand your social network and find more like-minded people who share your interests.

Here's how to attract and manifest the kind of pals you're looking for by using the power of the planets. Each is symbolic of a different kind of friend. You can either call on all the planets, as in the spell below, or just single out the 'types of friendship' you're looking for and call only on those planets associated with that type of friend. To do this, call on the appropriate planet using its associated incantation (see below), and repeat at each of the four directions – first to the north, then east, then south, then west. Finally, turn to the north, and bow to seal your intention.

* The moon brings you caring, gentle, intuitive souls.
* The sun attracts lively, dynamic, dramatic friends.
* Venus represents luxury-loving, warm-hearted, creative types.
* Jupiter represents independent, adventurous, spontaneous pals.
* Mercury encourages chatty, fun-loving, analytical people.
* Mars attracts sporty outgoing types, leaders and instigators.
* Saturn represents reliable, serious, introverted, down-to-earth pals.
* Neptune attracts dreamers, artists, musicians and spiritually enlightened types.
* Uranus brings innovative, humanitarian and eco-friendly souls.
* Pluto encourages deep thinkers, secretive souls and beneficially powerful pals.

1. On the evening of a full moon, cast a magic circle in your sanctuary (see p. 120) and stand facing north.

2. Raise your arms above your head and call on the power of the moon for a true sense of belonging and comradeship, saying, 'Blessings to the moon. Please manifest kind and caring friends into my life.'

3. Next, turn to the east and call on the sun, saying, 'Blessings to the sun. Please bring light-hearted, dynamic pals to my world.'

4. Now for the inner planets (those closest to the sun, apart from the Earth).

5. Turn to the south and say, 'Blessings to Mercury, Venus, Mars, Jupiter and Saturn, bring me fun, adventure, independence, self-reliance and creativity, all to be found in my future friends.'

6. Finally, turn to the west and call on the outer planets (those furthest from the sun) and say, 'Blessings to Uranus, Neptune and Pluto, to bring me humanitarian pals, deep thinkers and spiritually enlightened friends.'

7. Drop your arms by your sides and, to seal your intention to the universe, simply bow to the north, east, south and west.

It won't be long before you will be meeting the kinds of friends you are looking for.

TALISMAN OF ACCEPTANCE AMONG FRIENDS

It's nice to be popular and liked within your social circle. In fact, it not only boosts self-esteem but being accepted for who you are means you can accept and love yourself better, too. This talisman can be taken with you wherever you go if you need to feel accepted, less shy and more confident or simply project who you are in the best possible way.

You will need:
* 3 orange tea lights
* A piece of pink opal (the stone of self-love and acceptance – but rose quartz is a good substitute if this is hard to find)
* 2 pieces of citrine or sunstone

1. Set the three tea lights in a horizontal line on your altar or table, with the pink opal in front of the middle candle, and the two pieces of citrine (or sunstone) in front of the other two.

2. Light the candles, and sit for a few minutes, focusing on the flames to calm and still the mind.

3. Touch the citrine/sunstone to the left and affirm: 'I am filled with the light of the sun, bringing joy wherever I go.'

4. Touch the citrine/sunstone to the right and say, 'I am filled with the joy of my spirit and accept who I am.'

5. Now pick up the pink opal and say, 'I accept me as I am, and others will accept me too. I hold this talisman to my heart, and it will remind me that I am unique, special and true.'

6. When you feel ready, blow out the candles.

Take the opal with you wherever you go as a talisman of self-love and to attract positive acceptance from all around you.

....

KEEPING FRIENDS

Friends often drift apart – perhaps you move to a different part of the country or abroad, and, as much as you try to keep close tabs on one another through social media or video calls, you can easily lose touch without in-person contact.

Try this spell if you want to keep a relationship going, no matter what – and if the other person has the same intention as you, then the next time you meet it will be like you've never been apart.

You will need:
* A gold tea light
* A map of the world or globe
* A ball of gold twine or thread

1. Preferably on a new-crescent-moon evening, light the candle and sit facing your map or globe.

2. With your finger, point to where your friend is now living, even if it's only 20 miles away from you, and say:
   > I see you here, as you see me.
   > Across the skies we'll stay so true,
   > The moon shines down on both us two,
   > And keeps us bound in harmony.

3. Now take your ball of twine and begin to wind it around the globe as if you're creating a larger ball of string, winding from side to side, up and down, crosswise and so on, until you've covered it all. If you're using a flat map, spiral the thread outwards from the centre, to cover the whole thing.

4. Leave the gold-threaded map or globe in place for one lunar cycle, then slowly remove the thread.

5. Relight the gold candle and say, 'With this magic thread we are connected. Wherever you or I shall go in the world, so mote it be.'

Your connection with this friend will be assured always.

Now that you have cast spells for friends and family, it's time to manifest prosperity and a little luck into your life.

CHAPTER ELEVEN

Manifesting Abundance, Luck and Prosperity

Love betters what is best.
William Wordsworth 1770–1850
(English poet)

Most of us feel we need more of something in our lives at one time or another – whether more money, more luck, more self-esteem or just more time to live life freely. Abundance comes to us in different ways, depending on what we actually seek. Rooted in an ancient Latin word meaning 'overflowing', abundance was associated with the cornucopia or 'horn of plenty' – a vessel containing bountiful fruits of the harvest, first seen in ancient Greek iconography and carried by the Greek god of Earth's wealth and riches, Ploutos.

ATTRACT RICHES WITH A PLOUTOS VISUALISATION

Most people would like a little more money. But unless you specify exactly how much more you want, you may well only get an extra penny. Where money is concerned, when you bless the gods or weave a spell, do make it very clear – write it down, speak it aloud – how much you want (and be realistic). Ploutos doesn't make choices based on who deserves what; he just gives randomly when he sees something has to be given – so the more specific you are, the more likely he'll notice. Here's a spell to align to his power.

You will need:
* A cinnamon incense stick or a green tea light

1. Sit somewhere quiet, where you won't be disturbed, and light either the incense stick or the tea light to maximise the power of abundance and to invoke Ploutos' powers.

2. Close your eyes, take a few deep calming breaths and find stillness.

3. Imagine you are walking through a magnificent cave deep within the Earth's surface, your torchlight shining on stalagmites and stalactites, and you hear water dripping among the rocks. On the ground, crystals glitter in a ray of sunlight that beams through a tiny crevice from the rocks above. As you stand beneath this ray of light, it fills you with a golden warmth. You feel wealthy in spirit and soul.

   Three huge selenite crystal wands stand upright in the middle of the cavern floor. You reach out for them. As you do so, you hear a voice whispering, 'The treasures you will find here are yours to take. Anoint these crystals three times and you will have what you so desire.'

In the distant gloom, you see the god Ploutos bejewelled in gemstones and crystals of the Earth. Magnificent and smiling, he points to the trickle of water that runs down the side of the rocks, then he is gone. You place your cupped hands under the running water and anoint the first selenium wand, then repeat twice more to consecrate the others. But as the last crystal is anointed, they all vanish, the light from the crevice disappears and you find yourself not in a cavern beneath ground, but in a garden of the upper world, filled with fruit, plants and trees. You realise that the treasures Ploutos promised are already before you – you need only open your witch's eyes to see that the greatest wealth is knowing what you truly want and visualising it before you.

4. Slowly, become aware of your breath, and come back to normal awareness. Wiggle your fingers and toes, open your eyes and recall how this visualisation helps you to see that wealth is not just about outer materialism, but inner richness and the hidden gems within you.

....

A CORNUCOPIA FOR MANIFESTING WEALTH

If you do really want to attract pure material wealth into your life, this simple cornucopia jar will encourage it to you. You can use anything you like to fill up your cornucopia, as long as you have a good mix of 'wealth' correspondences, as outlined below.

You will need:
* A large jar or container with a lid
* A handful of coins, silver or gold items or images of money
* A handful of dried money herbs, such as mint, sage, basil and bay
* A selection of green and yellow crystals
* A few drops of sandalwood essential oil
* Green ribbon

1. Fill your jar or container with your coins, herbs and crystals and sprinkle the sandalwood oil over the items.

2. Close the jar and tie the green ribbon around it to seal your intention for a plentiful life.

Leave the jar in the southwest area of your home to attract prosperous people and encourage material gain.

....

BAY LEAF MONEY CHARM

The bay tree (*Laurus nobilis*) was prized by the god Apollo and has long been associated with wisdom, courage and status. One Greek myth tells how, pursued by Apollo, the nymph Daphne rejected him. She pleaded with her father (the river god Peneus) to save her, so he turned her into a bay tree. Apollo could only mourn his loss by wearing a crown of bay leaves, and dedicated the leaves to those who achieved the highest accolades in Greek civilisation. In Roman times, the bay tree became a status symbol of warriors and illustrious statesmen, and in folklore carrying a bay leaf in your purse or pocket was said to attract money.

This simple spell will also attract money, but only if you ask for exactly how much you are seeking and *truly believe that it is already yours*.

You will need:
* A pin or needle
* 3 bay leaves
* Frankincense essential oil

1. With the needle or pin, scratch on each leaf the amount of money you require (be realistic), and also your name in the remaining space.

2. Drop a little of the oil on to each leaf and say three times in total:
   > Oh, bay leaf true please send to me,
   > This money that is mine to be,
   > Bring me what is good and fair
   > And all that's meant for me out there.

3. To seal your intention, keep the leaves in your wallet or purse.

When the time is right, the amount you have asked for will manifest – so be patient!

....

MONEY AFFIRMATION SPELL

Below are nine different affirmations to attest that you already believe you have the money or prosperity you are seeking. Repeat them every day, three times in the morning, three times in the afternoon and three times in the evening, for nine days.

You will need:

✴ A piece of malachite, green aventurine or other green crystal

1. Take your crystal at the three times of day, and repeat each of the following lines three times:
   - I believe prosperity is mine.
   - I believe I am worthy of financial gain.
   - Wealth is drawn to me.
   - I'm receptive to all the abundance life offers me.
   - I do what I love and so prosperity flows to me.
   - Money comes easily into my life.
   - I receive all with gratitude and respect.
   - My positive attitude attracts prosperity.
   - I am empowered and motivated to make money.

2. After nine days, seal your intention to the universe by burying the green crystal at the foot of a tree to promote the financial reward you are seeking.

If you thoroughly believe prosperity is already yours, out there in the universe and ready to flow to you, it won't be long until you see the results you are looking for.

....

TREE POWER CHARM

Many trees are associated with prosperity. For example, the oak with long-term investment, economic reward or property negotiations; the rowan with successful enterprises; and the willow with positive business negotiations. In fact, trees generally are associated with material and financial empowerment, and can be used to encourage all-round abundance.

This spell, usually performed during a tree's dormant phase (in winter, for most deciduous trees) will mature your intention as the spring arrives, and its power increases in your favour as the tree develops and grows throughout the rest of the year. It will continue to manifest its benefits in years to come.

You will need:
* 3 x 90cm (or longer) pieces of natural twine/raffia (enough to tie around your chosen tree trunk)
* 9 stems from a bush or of a favourite flower (if you have to prune the bush, just graciously ask the plant if it's ok to do so first, and thank them after)

1. Choose a tree in your local environment – one to which you can return to reconnect to its power and revitalise your desire for abundance.

2. Take the first length of twine and tie it very loosely around the base of the tree, and then the second length about 20cm above the first and the third one 20cm higher.

3. Take your nine stems and weave each one vertically through the three twines, over and under and over, so the stems are equidistant around the tree trunk. (Don't worry if the stems are disturbed or the twine breaks in the days to come, as it is the actual spell that matters.)

4. Stand back and say:
   With twines and stems to you I'm bound,
   Where all my prosperous dreams be found.

> I bow to your spirit uplifting my strength,
> And your sacred power to bring me such wealth.

5. Bow to the tree, perhaps placing a stone or pebble as a token of your love for it at the base of the trunk, then return home.

6. One lunar cycle later, return to the tree and cut the binds (if they haven't already broken) to show your respect for the tree's growth.

The powerful connection you have forged will bring you opportunities for prosperity throughout the year. Return whenever you can to say thanks to your tree and, to revitalise its blessings, stand beneath it for a few minutes with your hands upon the bark, until you feel intuitively the moment is right to leave.

....

GREEN MAN OR HORNED GOD MAGICAL CHARM

Another favourite deity for replenishing the coffers or simply to invite prosperity into your life is the Horned God, often depicted as Cernunnos (god of the forest) and also identified with the Green Man. By calling on the god to join in your charm, you will be rewarded with his gifts of peace, wealth and wisdom.

You will need:
* A green tea light
* Frankincense essential oil
* A gold coin or ring
* An image of Cernunnos/Green Man or Horned God

1. Light the green tea light.

2. Drop a single drop of the essential oil on to the coin or ring to affirm your intention for wealth.

3. Gaze at your chosen image and say:

> The god of prosperity does see me this time,
> To bring me the gifts of a wealth that is mine.
> With green candle bright and a coin (ring) that is spun
> With frankincense fine now
> My spell work is done.
> Thank you, Cernunnos, so mote it be.

4. Place the coin on the image and leave overnight.

In the morning, place the coin in a pouch and keep this under your bed to promote prosperous living.

....

ATTRACT POSITIVE LUCK

Based on a mediaeval witch's spell, this charm draws on the spirits of the four winds or directions and was traditionally performed just after a new crescent moon. It was believed that the spirits of the north, south, east and west could blow fortune in your direction if you were perfectly aligned with their powers.

Perform this spell during a waxing phase of the moon.

You will need:
* A white tapered candle

* A little patchouli oil
* A piece each of malachite, red carnelian, citrine and blue lace agate

1. Anoint the candle with the oil by rubbing it down one side, then light the candle.

2. Place the four crystals in a circle around the candle to represent the points of a compass, with malachite to the north, red carnelian to the south, citrine to the east and blue lace agate to the west.

3. Say aloud:

   > By north and south and east and west,
   > These winds they blow me all that's best
   > Of goodness, luck and fortune, too,
   > I bless these spirits make it true.

4. Sit quietly for a few moments, until you are still and centred, then, when you feel ready, blow out the candle and take up the crystals.

Keep the crystals under your bed or pillow until the full moon to activate positive fortune into your world, then keep them in a safe place and they will remain charged with good-luck power.

....

NINE – KNOT FORTUNA SPELL

Fortuna, goddess of fortune in Roman mythology, was capricious in that the luck she distributed could be both good and bad. So the key to this spell is to make it clear that you are asking for favourable luck, so that when she knocks at your door she will bring the right type and scatter her positive energy all around you.

Knot spells are renowned for their power to 'bind' or 'tie in' intentions and seal desires (although some require you to 'untie' the knot, too, letting the energy disperse freely).

You will need:
* 3 x 60cm lengths of gold cord/twine
* 3 x 60cm lengths of red cord/twine
* 3 x 60cm lengths of green cord/twine
* 3 mint leaves (fresh or dried)

1. On the evening of a waxing moon, braid three separate plaits with gold, red and green cord or twine in each.

2. Knot off the ends and make a knot in the middle of each braid (so that's three knots per braid).

3. Slip a mint leaf into the middle knot of each braid.

4. Lay the plaits vertically in front of you, and say, 'With these nine knots, I ask for goodness, Fortuna: three for beneficial luck, three for happiness, three for gratitude and all for your kindness. So mote it be.'

5. Leave your petition in place until the following full moon, then return to finalise your spell.

6. Remove the three mint leaves, and begin to untie all your knots, in the following order: start with the one at the top, then the bottom one and then the middle one.

7. Once you have unknotted the braids, unwind them, until you have nine separate lengths of cord or twine again. Now say, 'These knots of intention for good luck are now unbound, so that I may benefit from their far-reaching power. Thank you, Fortuna, for this good luck, which is mine to have.'

8. Hang your ribbons or twine on your altar or on the inside of your front door or anywhere they can radiate their good-luck charm.

Every full moon, to maximise positive luck in your life, take the nine lengths of cord in a bunch and hold them between your hands while you say, 'Thank you, Fortuna, for this good-luck charm.'

....

BASIL AND TRIPLE-GODDESS OPPORTUNITY SPELL

Basil is a well-known cure-all, used in many spells for success, luck and love; and, like bay leaf, it can attract wealth if you carry a leaf in your wallet, or place it in the drawer of your desk to manifest good business dealings.

The following lunar charm will encourage opportunities to make more money, whether through luck, chance or sheer dedication to a desire for a certain amount.

You will need:
* A pen or pencil and paper
* 3 basil leaves (fresh or dried)
* 3 green tea lights

1. During a new-crescent-moon or waxing-moon phase, draw the Triple Goddess symbol on your piece of paper.

2. Lay a basil leaf on each of the moons – first one to the left, then one to the right, then one in the middle.

3. Light the three tea lights, place them in a line behind your symbol and say:

   > With basil three and Triple Goddess,
   > I light my way to fortune's fortress,
   > Where chance and luck will come my way
   > By Luna's power for me this day.

4. Close your eyes and meditate for a few moments on what good fortune means to you, and what good luck you would like to come into your life.

5. When you are ready, open your eyes and blow out the candles.

6. Remove the first basil leaf and place it underneath the first tea light. Leave the petition in place until the full moon.

7. Return to your spell on the full moon and remove the second basil leaf and place it under the second candle.

8. Relight the candles and repeat the spell, only this time say, 'With basil two . . ', etc.

9. Again, focus on opportunities and chances you are hoping for, and then blow out the candles.

10. Finally, just before or on the evening of the dark of the moon, perform the same spell, this time removing the last basil leaf from the centre and placing it under the third candle.

11. Repeat the spell, saying, 'With basil one . . .'

12. Once you have concentrated on your intention for a few moments, blow out the candles, place your finger in the middle of the now-empty Triple Goddess symbol and say, 'Thank you, moon goddess, for the goodness that is mine.'

By the next full moon, the chances you have been waiting for will be encouraged to manifest.

....

MONEY–ON–ITS–WAY SPELL

This spell requires patience and practice, as you have to make some repetitive gestures daily over a period of nine days and truly engage in the process of drawing money to you. With the help of lodestones (or magnetite – magnetic stones that attract good fortune to you if used in the correct way), you will achieve your money-making goal.

You will need:
* 2 green tea lights
* 2 lodestones (magnetite)

1. Light the tea lights and place the two lodestones 20cm apart on your altar or table in front of the candles, well enough away for safety.

2. Focus on the two candles for a moment, and say, 'Thank you, universe, for what I have already received is mine. So mote it be.'

3. Blow out the candles and leave in place.

4. Each day for nine days, light the candles and say the following, while visualising the amount of money or wealth you imagine is already yours:

> By the will of my intent
> Money comes, it's heaven sent.
> In abundance, nine times more,
> I see it coming through the door.
> Nine days, then the lodestones move
> Bringing all I hold is true.

5. Each day, move the lodestones a little closer together. When they touch (and you should ensure this happens on the ninth day), you will have sealed your intention to the universe.

Leave the stones in place for one lunar cycle before removing them to release the energy to the universe, knowing that what you have asked for is on its way.

. . . .

BEECH SPELL TO ATTRACT HELPFUL PEOPLE

In folklore, the beech tree, also known as the 'Queen of the Woods', is associated with wisdom, written knowledge, prosperity and wish fulfilment. Paper-thin slices of beech bark were used to make the earliest books, and mediaeval lovers believed that the higher you carved your

213

name on a beech tree on midsummer's night, the sooner you would be married. In British folklore, a wish inscribed on a beech stick planted in the ground would come true, and carrying small pieces of bark in your pocket was thought to attract good luck and success.

Use this simple spell to attract beneficial people who can help you to manifest all your financial goals. You can also use it to help sort out everyday money problems, such as finding help to pay off small debts, successful applications for a loan and so on.

You will need:
* 6 beech leaves (or 6 beech-leaf images)
* A piece of paper and a pen

1. On the evening of a waxing moon, draw a fairly large pentagram on your paper.

2. In each star point, write a word that sums up your current dilemma – such as loan, debt, benefactor, bank and so on. You can either use the same word five times or you can form a sentence using five words (one for each point). You will know what this refers to, but the universe does not, so make it as precise as you can – for example, 'Help pay off my loan'. In the middle section of the pentagram, write one word that sums up your goal.

3. Gaze at your pentagram and clearly ask out loud for what you need to help you out. Repeat five more times and then place a beech leaf (or image) in each of the points to cover the words and the sixth in the middle.

Leave until the next new moon, and your desire for financial help will be encouraged to manifest.

214

Manifesting prosperity doesn't usually happen overnight (unless you are lucky enough to have a windfall), but, with self-belief and confidence in your spells, you will encourage all the good luck and abundance you truly need into your world.

CHAPTER TWELVE

Manifesting Ambition, Success and Career Goals

*Do not follow where the path may lead. Go instead
where there is no path and leave a trail.*
**Ralph Waldo Emerson, American
philosopher, essayist and poet**

Most people have ambitions for some kind of personal success. You may wish to build a business empire, long for a simple, back-to-nature life or want to make a vocation out of your creative talent. Whatever your lifestyle goals, here are some spells to help you manifest them.

....

MANIFESTING AMBITIONS THROUGH THE ZODIAC (ACCORDING TO NORTHERN HEMISPHERE SEASONS)

If witchcraft seems heavily biased towards working with the cycles of the moon, think again – because, in fact, performing spells according to the sun's apparent path around the ecliptic (the imaginary belt made up of the twelve signs of the zodiac) can boost and promote aspects of the particular success you're looking for.

The sun in astrology represents our direction, our will and our desire for recognition or acclaim, and, as it moves through each sign, the energy changes and corresponds to certain qualities that the modern witch can use to invoke, summon and conjure up achievement.

Here's a guide to each of the zodiac sign energies to help you decide what action to take and when. There are no *prescribed* spells here; simply work with the knowledge you have acquired so far and refer to the Correspondence List on p. 275 to help you. I've included various symbols, colours or ingredients to inform a more personal choice, so you could, perhaps, light a candle for atmosphere and/or spread seasonal items, flowers or objects on your altar or table. Be creative with your wishes and desires, and write them down in your journal, along with the date of your spell and its progress. And always give thanks – to the universe for being there for you, and to your inner witch for her wisdom and connection to all of nature.

When the sun is in Aries (c. 21 March–20 April)

As the first sign of the zodiac, Aries is a raw, vital, exciting energy. There is a feeling of impetus, action and vibrancy. It's a get-up-and-go, no-nonsense, risk-taking time, and it asks us to take a few leaps and bounds, get motivated and be brazen and fearless.

So during this period, cast spells concerning leadership ambitions, winning a race, getting yourself into a prominent role; for short-term missions, beating a rival, setting up a new business or taking a gamble on a new direction.

Incorporate red into your spells, with candles, crystals (such as red carnelian and red jasper), vibrant or spicy botanicals (such as cinnamon and nutmeg) and give thanks to the ruler of Aries, the planet Mars, for its fiery joy and the god Ares for his courageous will to succeed.

When the sun is in Taurus (c. 21 April–20 May)

There is now a feeling of lush growth, as the sun moves higher into the sky and perennial plants and seedlings begin to emerge. Taurus, ruled by Venus, is about self-indulgence, care and attention to detail and our true values. So it's a time for creativity with your ideas – giving seed to them, but also deciding what your true aims are. This energy asks you to be realistic, take a look at your gifts, talents and what might give you a sense of security in the long term.

While the sun is in Taurus, perform spells that will encourage your creativity and those that involve you in practical projects and ways to indulge in the arts or the finer things of life. All careers or work ambitions concerned with pleasure, love, nature, craft and art and leisure are highlighted during this time.

Incorporate earthy colours into your spells, with green and brown candles, malachite and other green crystals; use fragrant botanicals (such as rosemary, oregano and Venus-ruled roses or rose essential oils and fragrances by the jar-load). Give thanks to Venus, for her gifts of self-love and appreciation for your creative skills.

When the sun is in Gemini (c. 21 May–20 June)

As the sun moves higher in the sky (in the northern hemisphere) a bubbly, carefree and light-hearted energy moves us into longer hours of daylight. With versatile Mercury ruling Gemini, there is also a growing realisation that we need a little more rational thinking and a lot less second guessing or overthinking. It's time to lift our mood and take a more light-hearted approach to life. The first signs of summer spring to life and the longer days cheer us all.

219

THE MODERN WITCH'S BOOK OF MANIFESTATION

This is the period for communicating your ambitions, making new contacts, networking, getting on whatever social or media platform is necessary. Cast spells to achieve short-term goals and propel long-term projects, to get you admiration and attention, boost your powers of persuasion or sell yourself and your ideas.

Incorporate yellow, white and gold into your spells. Place fresh sprigs of seasonal yellow flowers (say, daisies or a vase of dandelions) on your altar. Use citrine, opals and clear quartz crystals to bring panache to your spells and thank the god Hermes for his fast wit and magic touch in all negotiations.

When the sun is in Cancer (c. 21 June–22 July)

As the sun moves into Cancer to mark the summer solstice, this is the highlight of the Wiccan sun god's year, a celebration of light and joy. The summer is truly upon us as wayside plants bloom profusely, covering narrow lanes with trails of wild flowers, cereal crops tower dramatically over the once-stark earth and love is in the air.

This is a time to perform spells associated with making a long-term commitment, finalising projects or grabbing an opportunity that may have been open to you but you couldn't decide whether to take it or not. Now you can be sure, if you work with your intuition and forge a connection to nature. The energy of the actual solstice passes quickly, but while the sun is in Cancer you can discover a role or career where you feel you truly 'belong'.

Incorporate empowering lunar-associated crystals, such as moonstone, selenite and pearls; use sensual essential oils, such as ylang ylang and oud, to invoke deep emotional and spiritual connection to the Earth and the power of the moon. Thank the moon goddess, Selene, for lighting up the darkness to show you the way.

When the sun is in Leo (c. 22 July–20 August)

When the sun is in vitalising and fiery Leo, we are filled with energy-boosting self-empowerment and a spirited feeling that we're on top of the world. Summer is at its height, and, even if flowers begin to wilt in the hot sun, or holidays are taken in exotic locations, this is the perfect time to show ourselves off to the best possible advantage.

Leo is a sign of theatre, drama and showing off your talents, so, if you're up for celebrity status, a high-profile job or you simply want to create new strategies for success, it's time to kick-start your talents. This is the time for the first harvest, so it's opportune to also reap a few rewards from the spells you cast a few months back.

Incorporate sun-loving crystals, such as sunstone and tiger's eye, and the colours gold, orange and hot red to enhance all spell work. Scatter sunflower seeds or marigolds and red-hot chilli peppers across your altar to invoke the beneficial energy of the sun god. Use essential oils such as frankincense and wild orange to bring you confidence and determination. Thank the sun for its life-giving power and the gods Helios (the sun) and Apollo (god of light) for their magical influence in lighting your world.

When the sun is in Virgo (c. 21 August–20 September)

As summer draws to a close in the northern hemisphere, it brings a calmer, more studious atmosphere. The natural world sees the first harvest, and for us it's a time to sort the realistic possibilities from the pipe dreams. Virgo energy is cultivated and discriminating, so this is the perfect opportunity to 'check out' new business ventures, courses of study and training; it's also a time to for us to take a step back and analyse options and prioritise work–life balance and to consider the kind of lifestyle we truly seek.

Peridot is the crystal associated with Virgo, bringing clarity about future needs. Use it in spells to shed realistic light on the pathway before

221

you. Add cool, earthy colours (moss, sage green and ochre) or essential oils such as clary sage, sandalwood or cedarwood to ground your ideas. Use fresh herbs like dill and fennel to purify and declutter your mind. To encourage positive communication with others, call on the gods Mercury or Hermes in your spell work.

When the sun is in Libra (c. 21 September–20 October)

The autumn equinox at 0° Libra marks the day when astrological autumn begins. Summer has ended, and the autumn brings morning mists, falling leaves and a time to redress the balance of the year and give thanks for the joy of the harvest.

When the sun is in Venus-ruled Libra, cast spells concerned with careers or work involving design, art, aesthetics, justice, beauty and all forms of diplomacy. This is a time when you can 'attract' attention, and 'be' at your most charismatic. If you're looking for promotion or a business partner, this is the perfect opportunity to perform spells to enhance all aspects of negotiation.

Use Venusian motifs in your spells, such as doves and roses and sensual oils, such as rose and jasmine to enhance your attraction factor for head-hunting, getting on with new contacts or sending off applications. Sprinkle your altar with rose petals and carry or wear lapis lazuli for deep insights into your true ambition and sapphire to bring you success.

When the sun is in Scorpio (c. 20 October–20 November)

As the sun sinks lower towards the horizon, chilly mornings arrive, the days suddenly seem shorter and there is a sense that the natural world is slowing down (in the northern hemisphere). With the Samhain celebration on 31 October, we give thanks to the spirit world, and all that has been in both our ancestral past and this year. While the sun is in Scorpio, we are reminded that the upper Earth has been abandoned by the goddess of the underworld, Persephone. Nature now waits for winter to come and go and for her return in the spring.

Yet this is the perfect time to cast spells to reveal secrets, perform undercover work, check out who can and can't be trusted, reveal hidden talents, infiltrate new groups or eavesdrop on people in power to help you on your way. Scorpio is also about passion and money, so perform spells to enhance financial power.

Incorporate malachite for grounding and black stones, such as obsidian and tourmaline, to protect you from negativity. Use light green, dark blue and black candles, burn sandalwood and frankincense incense to enhance all spells concerned with self-promotion. Call on the all-seeing powers of the gods Hades and Ploutos for making calculated choices for the future.

When the sun is in Sagittarius (c. 20 November–20 December)

Metaphorical arrows fly when the sun is in Sagittarius. Although we will soon be experiencing the shortest daylight hours, and winter may be dark, gloomy, cold and damp, warmth comes from home fires and the promise of the imminent change of season, when the new sun god is born to the world. This anticipation heightens our mood – there is a sort of 'get-under-the-duvet' feeling, but also a renewed optimism, and an impatience for better things. Sagittarius is therefore about new hope in the darkness, a springboard for success, a time to take opportunities, seize adventure, set off on travels or take a chance on being in the right place at the right time.

Use Jupiter's powers of persuasion to get you further up any professional or social ladder or simply to get yourself around the globe. Add cedarwood, bergamot and wild orange oils to your spell work, not forgetting spices such as cinnamon, chilli, turmeric and nutmeg. Carry turquoise and green aventurine for luck and, as Sagittarius is the ninth sign of the zodiac, cast spells nine times more than the nine times you usually do to manifest an intention. This key manifestation number will multiply its empowering influence.

When the sun is in Capricorn (c. 21 December–19 January)

The sun's move into 0° Capricorn not only marks the winter solstice, but also the beginning of the festive season. The darkest days of deep winter are upon us, as we cosy up in families if we can and join in with merriment, whether religious or pagan celebrations for Yule. Capricorn is the sign of determination, achievement, conviction and stamina, so this is the perfect time to prepare and hone our 'career tools' for the calendar year ahead.

Use Saturn's disciplined energy to cast spells for self-empowerment. You can benefit from this period of laying down tools by finding time for deep reflection about your true goals. Perform spells that encourage you to take care of yourself, and also to build up your professional profile or image. Nurture your talents, give life to your qualifications and make use of your contacts. Or simply promote your own self-reliance and standing.

Incorporate crystals such as black tourmaline for grounding, garnet and rough rubies for self-belief and tiger's eye for self-assurance; use brown or orange candles, and earthy essential oils, such as patchouli, sandalwood and oud – not only to enhance your sensuality and give grace to your individuality, but also to encourage the riches of the Earth into your life.

When the sun is in Aquarius (c. 20 January–19 February)

Slowly but surely, there is a little more light every day, and the world around us is gradually coming back to life now. Winter aconites appear among the dead leaves, and we begin to feel a growing optimism in the air.

Aquarius is a sign of surprises, innovation and the unusual, so this is the perfect time to cast spells to manifest brilliant insights, creative channels and inventive new ways to make a living, or simply to think differently. It's also beneficial for attracting humanitarian and ecological work, for being a fashion trailblazer, for setting the world alight with avant-garde or nonconformist ideas and for literally changing the status quo.

Work with aquamarine, calcite, goldstone and azurite to help with interviews, mental clarity and negotiation. Use green candles and bergamot or wood-based essential oils in spells to boost originality and ground-breaking thinking.

When the sun is in Pisces (c. 19 February–20 March)

The last sign of the zodiac is, in astrological terms, the end of the solar cycle. We have come full circle and return to the fiery realm of Aries and the forthcoming spring equinox. Plants are coming to life, crocuses, daffodils, tulips and bluebells suddenly appear through the damp earth and the days are gradually getting longer.

This is the time to listen or attend to your dreams. A time when you can draw more easily on your creativity, longings, deepest intuition and cosmic connection. You can align with the watery world of fantasy, escapism and spiritualism and, if you are open to listening to your soul voice within, you will be surprised by how rewarding this 'otherworldly' knowledge can be.

During this period, cast spells to connect you to your imagination and the spiritual realms. Open yourself to the unbelievable, free yourself from the constraints of what you 'ought' to be and discover what or who you actually are. There are no rules or boundaries for Pisces, so this is your chance to feel boundless and, in doing so, to be at one with the infinite nature of the universe.

Decorate your altar with the first flowers of spring, like bluebells, and with blue crystals, like amethyst and blue lace agate, to help connect you to your spiritual self. Call on Neptune, both the god and the planet, to steer you through the waters of self-doubt or free you from others' expectations. This is a time to feel comfortable with being true to your witchy intentions, no matter who you are or what you believe, as long as you don't harm anyone else in the process – including yourself.

I suggest creating a journal or Book of Shadows specifically for these long-term monthly intentions and practices associated with the solar cycle. When you look back on your notes in the coming months, it will become clear to you what you were able to manifest and when. You can then use that knowledge again in future seasonal cycles.

Next up is a range of spells to manifest all those ambitions or career goals you long to achieve.

....

WITCH'S ALPHABET FOR SUMMONING SUCCESS

Commonly referred to as the Witch's Alphabet and often used by Wiccans to write secret messages, spells or charms, this alphabet was previously known as the Theban alphabet (named after Honorious of Thebes, a mythical mediaeval character). The script was first conceived by the occultist and cryptographer Johannes Trithemius and published in 1518, two years after his death.

When this 'secret' script is written by hand and coupled with the power of your intention, you can be assured of achieving the success you seek, particularly if you have a specific outcome in mind.

Only perform this spell on the evening of a waxing crescent moon, and have your precise intention ready.

You will need:
* A red tea light
* A piece of citrine
* A pen and paper
* A pouch or sachet

1. Light the tea light, and place the citrine beside it.

2. Using the witch's alphabet, as shown in the illustration above, write on your paper your name, then the charm – 'These magic words send me what I desire . . .' – followed by a sentence saying what it is you are hoping for. If you're new to this form of writing, it might take some time, but that's actually a good thing – because pen-to-paper writing is thought to be magical in itself, and the effort and focus involved will bring your imagined outcome to life on the paper.

3. Place the citrine on the paper and leave overnight, then blow out the candle.

4. The next day, fold the paper around the crystal and put them in your pouch or sachet.

Keep the pouch in your pocket or bag and carry with you wherever you go. Success will be yours if you truly believe in the words you have written.

....

OAK CHARMS FOR EMPOWERMENT

Oak trees are revered among witches for their magical powers. Whenever you come across one of these magnificent trees – even a young one – its strength and endurance are immediately evident; you can sense its majesty and empowering energy just by leaning against its trunk.

Whether you gather its acorns or fallen leaves in winter or simply draw, paint or find images of the oak, it is an essential ally and power booster for all forms of business, career and lifestyle spells. (You can collect oak leaves and acorns, when available, and keep them in a special box to use at other times of year.) Here are a few ideas for making use of the mighty oak.

* Carry an acorn in your pocket when you go to an interview or business meeting; it will bring you good luck.
* Lay out five oak leaves in the shape of a pentagram, with an acorn in the middle. Anoint the acorn with cedarwood essential oil and leave the arrangement near the main entrance of your home to attract success into your life.
* Visit a local oak tree (if you have none near by, you can visualise this spell instead). Stand with your back against the trunk for a few

minutes and, being realistic, meditate on your most fundamental goal, really believing that you are going to manifest this change (and when). As you lean against the trunk, repeat your commitment to engaging in this process nine times, then take a break and repeat another nine times and so on, until you have said it eighty-one times in all. Then leave the tree, turn, bow and give thanks to it. The changes you are seeking will begin to manifest with the mighty oak's strength and support.

* First thing in the morning of Beltane, go outside and capture some dew in the palm of your hand from among the grass or plants around you. (You can also collect dew from a car windscreen.) Place the dew on the bark of an oak tree, as an offering to the Earth goddess, and she will help to grant your wish.

....

VOCATION OR CAREER ENCHANTMENT

There are times when we don't know exactly what we want, or what's for the best, especially if there are other people, family or relationships to consider.

So rather than rushing headlong into a spell, this charm gives you time to work through ideas and intentions, to add and subtract, mix and match and generally reflect on your deepest desires before acting on any of them. It's also the perfect way to keep tabs on your short-term goals if you're someone who likes to have lots of them on the go all at once.

You will need:
* A red tea light
* A blackboard, thick card, mood board or canvas

* Scissors, pins, glue or sticky tape
* Pen, markers, crayons
* Cut-out images of leaves or fake or dried leaves
* A piece each of red carnelian and tiger's eye

1. Light the candle for ambience but keep it well away from your work-space for safety.

2. Assemble your vocation 'tree' by fixing your board, card or canvas to a wall or propping it up on an easel or somewhere it won't be disturbed. You could, perhaps, create a branching tree by drawing lines out across the canvas or board.

3. Either write your intentions directly on the leaves or images or paste words on to them.

4. Prioritise your goals, placing the most pressing, essential or long-term ones at the top of the tree, and the least important or more attain-able ones lower down.

5. Finally, place the two crystals in front of the tree, blow out the candle and leave the crystals and candle in place to encourage motivational energy each time you focus on your tree.

The leaves and words are visual reminders of what you want in life – but, of course, life can change, as do goals. So you can take down leaves and replace them with others, as and when. Growing all these ideas into existence is like growing any tree – it takes time, effort and engagement with the process. Even if your tree gets rather full, you will find that the fruit it bears will be the true fruits of your labour.

369 SPELL FOR PERSONAL SUCCESS

The numbers three, six and nine are often used in modern-day manifestation techniques. Here is a witch's spell to vitalise your motivation and bring it to life, along with the ability to fully believe in yourself and your goals.

You will need:
* A pen and paper
* A red tea light

1. Draw a large triangle on your paper.

2. Next to the north point, write 'Spirit'; at the bottom left point, write 'Soul'; and at the bottom right point, write 'Destiny'.

3. Place the candle in the centre of the triangle, light it carefully and focus on the flame for a few moments, while you repeat your intention nine times.

4. Then say, 'My Spirit, Soul and Destiny chosen, I offer this intention to the universe. So mote it be.'

5. Blow out the candle to seal your intention to the universe and keep your triangle in a safe place.

6. Finally, write down your intention daily three times in the morning, six times in the afternoon and nine times in the evening for thirty-three days (sorry!). Amplify your intentional phrase using positive

words and in the present tense, as if it's already appeared in your life. For example: 'I am really thankful for the universe aligning with me to attract fifty pounds into my life, bringing gratitude for all that is mine.'

You may well find that if you truly believe in what you are doing, you won't need thirty-three days to see results.

....

WHISPERED WORDS TO ATTRACT GOOD ADVICE

Whatever kind of success or acclaim you're looking for, you may find it hard to progress without the help of beneficial contacts, advisers and so on. To ensure you attract the right kind of mentors into your world, perform the following spell – but only when the wind or breeze is blowing from the north or northwest (the direction associated with career, progress and useful contacts).

1. Sit or stand facing into the north/northwest wind – preferably outside, where you can feel it blowing on your face.

2. Raise your arms towards the wind, as if to embrace it, and say, 'Come to me those who offer help and genuine support, and to you, too, will I bring support and dedicated love in return.'

3. Close your eyes and imagine a specific person (or type of person) – someone who could be of help/a mentor, or even someone famous who represents success to you in some way. Imagine them in a location of your choice.

4. Now visualise yourself as invisible to them, whispering in their ear. Say out loud to the wind what you want them to hear. For example, 'Please bring me support and advice' or, 'Please help me to achieve my goal' and so on.

5. Imagine yourself walking away from them, believing that this person will contact you. Then let go of the visualisation and open your eyes to face the wind.

6. Thank the wind for blowing the right type of help in your direction.

Watch out for the kind of helpful person you are seeking to come into your life in the weeks ahead.

....

KEY CHARM FOR A CHANGE OF DIRECTION

You can use a key to open a door to a new future or opportunity and also to close a door on the past, locking away what didn't work behind you. And keys can be symbols of thresholds and liminal places, where there is neither a future nor a past to consider, only the moment of change or transition.

Keys are also powerful symbols of locking and unlocking energy in witchcraft. This spell uses a real key to unlock your future and to lock the door on the past, so you can make the changes you truly want. Perform it on a full-moon evening.

You will need:
* A pen and paper
* A large metal key to represent 'now' (you might want to keep an old

233

vintage or pretty antique key with all your other witch paraphernalia, or hang one on your sanctuary wall as decoration)
* A black tea light (to represent the past)
* A red tea light (to represent the future)

1. Reflect on exactly what you want to change. A change of scenery? A change of job? Or perhaps a lifestyle change? A new way to find a work–life balance?

2. Write down the change you want to see on the piece of paper and place your key on top of it.

3. Light the two tea lights carefully, placing the black to the left, and the red to the right of the paper.

4. Gazing into the flame of the black tea light, say, 'I lock the door on past affairs that are no longer valid in my present,' then pick up the key and quickly pass it through the tip of the candle flame, being careful with your fingers.

5. Gazing into the flame of the red tea light, say, 'I unlock the door to the future to make the change I know is right for me now.' Pass the key quickly through the flame, then wait a minute for it to cool down, before placing it down on the paper.

Keep the key under your bed for one lunar cycle, and the changes you seek will begin to be set in motion by the following full moon.

KEEPING RIVALS AWAY MAGIC POUCH

As I've said before, we do not use witchcraft to harm others, nor to attempt to control them. However, there are times when we all need to protect ourselves from the bad feelings, envy, scorn, negativity or rivalry of others. This is particularly evident in the corridors of power, social media and business, where inflated egos are rife. The protection pouch in this spell will help you to protect yourself from all this.

You will need:
* A pen and paper
* A small piece of black tourmaline or obsidian
* A small organza pouch

1. Draw a pentagram on your scrap of paper.

2. Now draw the symbols for Fire, Earth, Air and Water at four of the points (see illustration, p. 00) and the word 'Spirit' beside the top point.

3. Underneath the pentagram, write your name and the words 'hen to pan'. This is an ancient magical Greek phrase meaning 'all is one'; it is associated with the ouroboros symbol (the snake eating its tail) – a sign of eternal protection.

4. Fold the paper around your stone and place it in the pouch.

Carry your magic pouch with you as a protective talisman against rivals and scoundrels, or keep it in your office or desk.

SPELL FOR MANIFESTING PROPERTY SUCCESS

Whether you're looking to buy a home, invest in property, win a sealed bid on a home or find the perfect place to rent, this spell will encourage positive results.

You will need:

* 3 keys
* Wild orange or cedarwood essential oil
* 3 pieces of malachite
* 3 green tea lights

1. Arrange the three keys in a three-pointed star, so that the unlocking parts all face inwards, touching in the middle.

2. Place a piece of malachite at the outer end of each key.

3. Release a single drop of oil on to each crystal.

4. Place the tea lights around the crystals, and then carefully light them.

5. As the flames flicker and burn, say:
   > Empowered I am, this deal be done.
   > With all belief, I'll find it won,
   > To bring me joy and then progress
   > This home's intention for success.

6. Focus on your intention – on exactly what you want to manifest. Visualise how it would feel to live there (or, if it's an investment,

what you hope it will allow you to achieve) and then blow out the candles.

The universe is now primed to bring you the results you truly desire.

From manifesting your practical needs, ambitions and career intentions, it's now time to turn to your personal wellbeing in the next chapter.

CHAPTER THIRTEEN

Manifesting Wellbeing According to the Seasons

Three winters cold
Have from the forests shook three summers' pride,
Three beauteous springs to yellow autumn turn'd
In process of the seasons have I seen . . .
Shakespeare (Sonnet 104) 1564–1616
(English dramatist and poet)

There are many ancient and traditional ways in which we can boost, heal and restore ourselves, whether with lotions, potions, spells or rituals. But by working with your seasonal characteristics and associated symbols and correspondences (based on the time of year you were born and the sun's cycle), you can align with certain energies to nurture and reinforce holistic harmony, enhancing your wellbeing even more.

THE SPRING WITCH: SPELLS FOR WITCHES BORN BETWEEN SPRING EQUINOX AND SUMMER SOLSTICE (21 MARCH—20 JUNE)

You were born into a time of celebration of the sun climbing higher in the sky (in the northern hemisphere), when new life is bursting forth. This time of the year is associated with fresh ideas, action, creativity, a youthful, fun-loving spirit and indulgent self-pampering. So to manifest balance and harmony for your inner spring witch, try out the following spells.

Bathing beauty charm

To maintain your youth-like charm and outer vibrancy, scatter some rose petals, lavender and mint leaves across your bath. Add clary sage, ylang ylang or wild orange essential oils into the running water to enhance your spring-like charm and place a piece of citrine at each corner of your bath, to imbue yourself with the power of abundant tranquillity and a sense of positivity wherever you go.

Soul wellbeing

Outer beauty is one thing, but an inner sense of wellbeing is about nurturing your soul. Here's how . . .

You will need:
* 2 red tea lights
* 3 pieces of red carnelian
* Petals or leaves of marigold, geranium, rosemary, rose, oak (if necessary, substitute with what's in season)

1. On the eve of a new crescent moon, place the tea lights on a flat surface, and the three pieces of red carnelian between them.

240

2. Sprinkle the petals over the crystals, to bring harmony and balance to your springtime energy.

3. Just before sunset (the nearer you can do this to sundown, the better), hold each crystal in turn to your chest and say: 'I am of the spring, and of spring will I live with wisdom, vision, passion and optimism. May this clarity flow into others' hearts as well as my own, cleansing and vitalising my soul, mind and spirit, and refreshing my whole being.'

4. Place the crystals beside the candles and for a few moments reflect on how you are being vitalised, feeling in balance with yourself — body, mind and soul.

5. Blow out the candles.

Enjoy being the spring witch you are — you will now feel revitalised in mind, body and soul alike.

Restorative relaxation spell
Spring witches are so full of physical energy that they often find it difficult to relax and restore their spiritual self.

Do this spell on a full-moon day/evening to bring equilibrium to your body, so you can wind down, relax and float downstream, revived and ready to go again.

You will need:
* A pine cone
* A piece of citrine
* Sandalwood essential oil

1. Sit cross-legged (preferably outside) to ground yourself.

2. Place the pine cone and the citrine in front of you.

3. Take up the pine cone in both hands and hold it close to your navel.

4. Close your eyes and focus on the pine cone. Press your hands against its rough surface and feel it radiate empowering energy through you.

5. Open your eyes and release a single drop of sandalwood oil on to the citrine.

6. Take a deep breath and breathe in the woody aroma, now filling you with calm and peace.

Leave the pine cone and citrine near a window in your home to draw down the power of the moon and recharge and balance you with both vibrant energy and the calm of an early spring morning.

···

THE SUMMER WITCH: SPELLS FOR WITCHES BORN BETWEEN SUMMER SOLSTICE AND AUTUMN EQUINOX (21 JUNE – 20 SEPTEMBER)

Witches born into summertime are people lovers, thriving on adoration and praise. They are more aware of other people's energy levels than their own and truly care about making them feel warm, welcome and comfortable. Whether you are the kindly, mothering witch, the entertaining one or the wise, discerning sorceress, your summer strengths are about always being true to yourself and expressing your creative talents.

Inner-and-outer beauty spell

Marigolds symbolise summer sunshine and the joyful personality of the summer-born witch. They are perfect for adding to a luxurious bath-time spell, so the summer witch feels connected to their inner solar light, shining it out there into the big, wide world.

You will need:

* Marigold petals (enough to scatter both around your home and in your bath)
* 4 gold tea lights
* Some rose petals and lavender
* Ylang ylang or patchouli essential oil
* Bath oil of your choice

1. Sprinkle the marigold petals in all four directions in your home to maximise and balance your outer radiance.

2. Now prepare a sensual bath, placing a gold tea light at each corner and scattering marigold petals on the surface, along with the roses and lavender.

3. Add a little ylang ylang or patchouli essential oil to your chosen bath oil to stimulate compassion and gentleness and to give you a deeper connection to your sensual summery needs.

This spell trades worn-out patterns of behaviour for a more vitalised summery spirit, ensuring that your outer beauty is in harmony with your inner joyful self.

Self-esteem-boosting olive charm

Olives are known for their benefits for the digestive and circulatory systems. They are also used in magic spells for their symbolic power of integrity and self-confidence and align to the summer witch's need for compliments and admiration to boost self-esteem.

Place fresh olives (green or black – not soaked in brine, but oil is ok) or olive leaves in a bowl and put it by your front door to enhance positive thinking and attract praise and flattery. You can also incorporate olives into your diet, adding them to pizzas, pasta and any Mediterranean-style dish; or pop some red chillies into a bottle of olive oil, to be used at any time of year as a great tonic to revive your summer zing.

To manifest abundant wellbeing

This spell is best performed during your own summer season to amplify and connect to the energy within you and ensure that for the rest of the year ahead, you are balanced in mind, body and spirit, ready to perform your magic. Practise it on a still summer's evening or, even better, on your birthday.

You will need:
* A piece of peridot (represents the sign of Virgo)
* A piece of tiger's eye (represents the sign of Leo)
* A moonstone (represents the sign of Cancer)

1. Take the three crystals and sit somewhere comfortable outdoors.

2. Hold the peridot to your navel and relax, then take three long, deep breaths and ask the Horned God/Green Man to send you fertile, creative ideas all year round.

3. Next, take up the tiger's eye, hold it to your third-eye chakra (midway between your eyebrows) and ask the Earth Goddess to send you her wisdom, confidence and vitalising power all year round.

4. Finally, hold the moonstone to your chest and ask the lunar goddess, Selene, to bring you intuition and spiritual healing and enhance inner beauty all year round.

5. Thank the gods.

Keep the stones in a safe place and repeat every season of the summer witch.

THE AUTUMN WITCH: SPELLS FOR WITCHES BORN BETWEEN AUTUMN EQUINOX AND WINTER SOLSTICE (21 SEPTEMBER—20 DECEMBER)

Witches born at this time are on a quest to harvest ideas, reap the rewards of their fertile minds, venture forth, deepen their knowledge, share their ideas and find a meaning in life. They have an innate connection to the mystical world and can draw on hidden knowledge to help them divine the future. The autumn witch understands how the harvest marks the end of one season, but also begins another; the dark nights are drawing in, but they know how to work with this transitionary energy to prepare for the coming year.

Dandelion spell for vitality
Perform this dandelion spell to restore your inner vitality and joie de vivre whenever your wellbeing is in need of a boost.

Collect some dandelion seed heads in a paper bag (taking care not to let the seeds blow away when harvesting). The more you gather, the more you will be able to scatter your desire to the wind. On a breezy or windy evening, during a waxing-moon phase, take your bag outside and gently shake out the contents. As you watch the seeds rise and fall on the wind, imagine yourself travelling, moving, inspired and vitalised, following the seeds, as they find places to stop and take root. Each seed is a messenger sent out to nature for your wellbeing to be restored, so you're ready to take action in the forthcoming cycle.

Mint for outer beauty
Mint is associated with strength and wisdom, and is used to hydrate, soothe and tone the skin. This mint spell will boost the autumn witch's powerful outer glow and strengthen inner sagacity.

You will need:
* A glass bowl
* 2 pink tea lights
* A handful of mint leaves (any kind is ok)

1. On a full-moon night, fill your glass bowl with water and place it outside.

2. Place a tea light either side of the bowl. (You don't have to light them.)

3. Sprinkle the mint leaves over the surface of the water and affirm: 'I am a witch of the autumn and, for outer beauty and harmony of mind, body and soul, I dedicate this bowl to the goddess of the moon. With renewed serenity, I will be cleansed and vitalised within and out.'

4. If you lit the candles, blow them out, and leave the bowl outside overnight.

5. In the morning, pour the water, with the leaves, over both your hands.

You will be imbued with calming, healing energy, and all aspects of your intuitive self enhanced.

Leaf-fall spell

To benefit your holistic wellbeing (where body, mind and soul are working in harmony), it's important to get close to the source of who you are, and there's no better way than by engaging in the autumnal world echoing your birth.

Go for a walk one bright, breezy autumnal morning and watch the leaves beginning to fall. Perhaps stand for a few moments and observe, as they glisten in the sun or get caught on a breeze. Oak trees shed their leaves in groups, whereas birches often shed one at a time, like slowly drifting golden flakes, falling with grace. You too are of the autumn, when leaves fall. So if you can, catch a few falling leaves as you go about your walk. Marvel at their grace – because they reflect all elements of your inner beauty. When you get home, keep the leaves in a safe place to dry out, or even press them in your journal.

This simple spell will align you to the energy of the trees in autumn – your time, your moment to fall into yourself.

THE WINTER WITCH: SPELLS FOR WITCHES BORN BETWEEN THE WINTER SOLSTICE AND SPRING EQUINOX (21 DECEMBER—20 MARCH)

Among the dark is found the greatest light, and being born into winter and Yule time means you're the kind of witch who can see deeply into other people's souls. You're serious about life, love and manifesting your dreams because you know how cold it can be, chilling bones and freezing hearts. Winter witches have resilience, incredible insight and spiritual awareness.

A bath-time spell
Whenever you have the opportunity, try this indulgent, sensual bath and you will feel revived, reawakened and more in touch with your feelings and what matters to you.

You will need:
* A white tea light
* Bergamot or wild orange essential oil

1. Light the tea light and place it at the head of your bath to represent distinction, individuality and self-respect.

2. Sprinkle a few drops of oil into your bath.

3. As you lie back, swish your hands around in the water and focus on the ripples, the reflection of the candle and how this is like you: the candle is your body, the ripples your aura radiating from you and the flame lighting your way.

4. Relax in the bath and say, 'I am a witch of winter, and with this flowing energy I pour creative love into the souls of all. My love is offered freely, with warmth and understanding, with integrity and dedication.'

5. Your circulatory system will be boosted and your nerves calmed. The bath will fight any self-doubt and boost self-confidence.

Feeling at one with the world

The winter witch accepts the cold of winter, but also yearns for the warmth of spring. Perform this spell on a full-moon night to feel at one with the world and to nourish your inner and outer wellbeing.

You will need:
* 5 moonstones
* A gold-coloured coin, ring or bracelet
* A metal, pewter or silver cup or goblet (or even a tin can)
* Clove essential oil (for warmth and grounding)
* 2 white tea lights

1. Arrange the moonstones in a circle.

2. Put the coin, ring or bracelet in the cup and place in the centre of the circle.

3. Sprinkle a little oil into the cup.

4. Light the tea lights, place them either side of the cup and affirm out loud, 'I am a witch of the winter, of nature's deepest heart and desire,

249

and I am her child. These stones I cast before me are treasures of myself; they are the gemstones of my inner warmth.'

5. Take up the moonstones and cast them into the cup.

Leave your petition in place until the following new moon, and you will feel restored and animated.

Mind and body in harmony

Midwinter's festive season is your season, too, so be generous and bountiful and give out the glow of your own inner witchy warmth all year round. For the rest of the year, this simple talisman will keep your body and spirit in balance, ready for your season to come around again.

You will need:
* 5 x 30cm lengths of gold ribbon (to represent the five golden elements of beauty within you)
* A piece of citrine
* A clear quartz crystal
* An image of a pentagram

1. Coil a golden ribbon into a circle in each of the pentagram points.

2. Place the citrine in the middle.

3. Sit for a few minutes and find calm and stillness. When you feel centred, focus on the citrine and say, 'I am cleansed and inspirited by this crystal's power, and my body will be as golden and glowing as these ribbons here beside me.'

4. Take the ribbons and knot them together (once at each end, and three equidistant knots between them).

5. Pick up the clear quartz and hold it close to your third-eye chakra for a few moments to connect this energy to the source of your inner witch.

Keep the knotted ribbons under your pillow for harmony of mind, body and soul.

Whichever season you were born into, using the spells in this chapter to pamper yourself in alignment with that time of year will restore and inspirit you with vitality and self-confidence, ready for the months ahead.

CHAPTER FOURTEEN

Manifesting Self-Empowerment, Inspiration and Adventure

If you don't know where you are going, any road will get you there.
Lewis Carroll, English author, poet and mathematician

This chapter looks at spells to manifest inspirational ideas and insights and to enhance all forms of creative thinking, as well as giving you the ability to advance your ideas, persuade others of your talents and get results. You can use them to inform and bring clarity to goal setting and to give yourself time to think before you act and stand firm in your priorities. The spells will also help you to plan new life directions and give you the courage to make important decisions for travel and adventure.

We are not all born travellers, although many of us have no choice but to travel far afield for work, family reasons or for a new start in life. Equally, some of us yearn for adventure, or just want to take a year out from a routine existence to understand more about life and still have a home to come back to. And others are in no need of a physical home, as they carry the essence of 'home' in their minds.

Whatever kind of traveller you are, the universe is there to help manifest your intention for a bon voyage, a more spiritual, inner journey or a lifestyle change.

....

BOUNDARY – CROSSING SPELL

When setting off on any new adventure – whether a massive lifestyle change, a trip to somewhere new or simply finding creative inspiration – the first hurdle is knowing how to get from that great thought inside your head to actually carrying it out.

Here's how to cross the threshold from your old life to your new one. This spell can also be performed for crossing any personal boundary, and moving into a better, more self-empowered place.

You will need:
* 7 red tea lights
* 7 stones, pebbles or shells

1. Place the tea lights in a circle on your altar or a safe, flat surface, and light them.

2. Arrange the stones in a well-spaced-out horizontal line on the ground in front of you and say, 'I now accept this chance to transform my life, and will cross the line, with all intention to fulfil [insert the 'change' you have in mind].'

3. When you feel centred and relaxed, take one step across the line of stones and imagine yourself crossing a life-changing boundary. Keeping one foot behind the line, in the past, and the other in front

of it, in the future, reflect on your desired change for a moment before repeating your affirmation.

4. Now take your back foot off the ground and place it beside the foot that is in the 'future'.

5. Say, 'I have now crossed the boundary of myself and am ready to make the changes manifest in my life. So mote it be.'

6. Finally, turn to face the red tea lights, and, when you are sure you have truly committed to this new direction, blow them out to seal your intention to the universe.

You have now stepped over to a new beginning and can move on from the past to the very beautiful future you so desire.

....

SELF-EMPOWERMENT PENTAGRAM SPELL

There are times when we all need to give ourselves a boost of confidence, empowerment and a sense of direction.

Try this spell every lunar cycle, if you like, or just when that feeling comes over you – maybe during an intuitive moment when you feel you need to check in with who you are and where you are going.

You will need:
* A piece of paper and a pen
* A moonstone

1. Preferably on the evening of a waxing moon, draw on your paper a row of five pentagrams, interspaced with five circles.

2. In each point of the pentagrams, write 'Self', and, in the centre, write the words 'I wish'.

3. In each circle, write as much as you can fit in (perhaps spiralling around the inside) about how exactly you would like to be empowered.

4. Fold the paper and place it where it will draw down the energy of the moon (a window ledge, for example) and put your moonstone on top of it.

5. In the morning, wrap the paper around the moonstone.

Keep the paper-covered stone with you for twenty-four hours (in a pocket, pouch or bag) and you will feel empowered and confident.

....

KEEP ME SAFE ON MY TRAVELS

Some spells require you to engage with the big, wide world, rather than performing them in the safety of your sanctuary. This magic oil will protect you from any negativity when out and about.

You will need:
* 2 large tablespoons almond oil (the carrier oil)
* 2 drops of rosemary essential oil
* 2 drops of cedarwood essential oil

* 2 drops of wild orange essential oil
* A small phial or bottle with dropper

1. Mix the oils directly in the phial and shake gently.

2. Hold the bottle in both hands, close to your body, and visualise the protective energy around you.

3. Say out loud: 'This magic unguent will protect me from all negativity whenever I go to practise my spell work.'

4. Dab a drop of the oil either on to each of your wrists or on a permeable stone of your choice (a good alternative if you are allergic) and reaffirm your intention by repeating the words in step 3 twice more.

Carry the stone with you in a pouch and you'll be safe on your travels.

....

ROWAN – TREE SPELL FOR FINDING YOUR WAY

The Greek goddess Hebe lost the magical chalice of nectar (which granted eternal youth to the gods) and was aided in retrieving it by an eagle. A rowan tree grew wherever the eagle's feathers fell, and the tree has thus become associated with the gift of youth, as well as with Hebe. In a later French mediaeval version of this tale, the helper was a hare, and his footprints were said to lead the way to the magic chalice, hidden beneath the rowan tree. In folklore, if you carried a branch of the rowan (also known as the wayfarer's or traveller's tree), you would never get lost and would be protected from evil.

With delicate, symmetrical leaves, the rowan produces vibrant red berries, the seeds of which are arranged in a natural pentagram shape, symbolising that the five elements of nature are with you wherever you go.

Use this rowan spell to avoid getting lost, both literally, on your travels, and emotionally. However, if you were to get lost, the rowan tree reminds you that in being lost, you often find a new direction.

If you happen to have a rowan growing near you, stand for a while with your back against its trunk and give thanks for its strength and protection. Take up a fallen leaf or twig (don't pull any off the branches) and take it to your altar. If there isn't a rowan near by, and you don't have the time to seek one out, find an image of one to use instead.

You will need:
* A fallen rowan twig or leaf (or an image of one)
* 5 red tea lights

1. Place your rowan twig, leaf or image on your altar.

2. Light the tea lights to symbolise the five elements and place them in a line behind the twig.

3. Place your hand on the twig and say:
      Oh, rowan tree, I thank you now
      To find my way through all and vow
      This way's not lost, my trust in you
      Will always find my way to truth.

4. Move the tea lights so that they encircle the twig and leave for a few minutes, while you find stillness and sense the power of the tree's protection.

5. When you feel ready, blow out the tea lights to seal your intention to the universe.

Now you can travel at ease in body or mind, and always find your way to a new direction or back to yourself.

....

TURQUOISE TO MANIFEST YOUR DESIRE FOR ADVENTURE

It was believed by the ladies of the Italian Renaissance courts that if, on your travels, you wore three turquoise stones between your breasts, you would never come to any harm, and the amazing blue–green stone is still renowned today for its magical powers of courage, goal setting, safe travels and inspiration. This simple spell will encourage the manifestation of your quest for adventure or a complete change of lifestyle.

You will need:
* A tea light
* 3 turquoise stones
* A pen and paper

1. Light your candle for atmosphere and imagine your future goal, travel plan, adventure or lifestyle challenge. Whatever it is, visualise being part of it – being there in the place itself and actually experiencing it.

2. After visualising this for a few minutes, take the three stones and place them in a triangle on your paper (with one point facing towards the top of the page, the other two facing the bottom left and right corners).

3. Draw in the lines of the triangle between the stones to link them up.

4. Now draw circles or swirls around the stones, or spirals or wavy lines around the whole triangle, letting your imagination talk through your hand, so that you are just doodling.

5. When you feel the moment is right, stop doodling and drop the pen. Crumple up the doodles and throw them away; you no longer need to dream – you can make this a reality!

6. Pick up the turquoise stones in your writing hand, hold them up to your third-eye chakra (midway between your eyebrows) and visualise your chosen adventure.

7. Blow out the tea light when you feel ready.

Keep the turquoise stones with you in a pouch or pocket for at least one lunar cycle and your future plans will manifest as you desire.

....

THE GREAT ADVENTURE TALISMAN

Many spells use keys, representing the unlocking or opening of doors, particularly those that lead to desirable outcomes. Use this one to open the door to opportunity and attract stimulating adventures all year round. You can also carry a specially 'charged' key wherever you go to feel self-empowered. Perform this spell on a waning-moon night.

You will need:
* 5 metal keys
* Sandalwood incense

1. Activate or 'empower' your keys with a little manifesting magic. Cleanse them by passing each one through the smoke of your sandal-wood incense.

2. Arrange the keys on a table or your altar in the shape of a five-pointed star, with the unlocking ends pointing outwards.

3. Leave the keys in place until the following waxing-moon period, then gather them together and hang them from a hook on a south-facing wall.

Your keys will bring all kinds of opportunities and exciting experiences according to your desires. Carry one chosen key with you (or the whole bunch, if you prefer), safely stowed away in a pouch or bag, to attract good luck on your travels.

You now have a collection of prescribed manifesting spells at your fingertips. The next step, if you so choose, is to create your own, and the following chapter will give you some basic tips for doing just that.

FIRE   EARTH   AIR   WATER   SPIRIT

CHAPTER FIFTEEN

Creating Your Own Spells

Great things are done by a series of
small things brought together.
Vincent van Gogh, Dutch painter

Spell weaving is a bit like knitting, embroidery or tapestry, in that you are threading together ideas, symbols and ingredients that 'work' in tandem to create a whole. So as mentioned previously, if you can't get hold of the ingredients specified in any of the spells in this book, you can draw on the Correspondence List on p. 275 to mix and match and choose your own. However, while I have given you a framework of traditional correspondences to work with, there's no harm in trying out your own recipes and spells, too. It is entirely up to you and this is one reason why recording things in a Book of Shadows or a journal is essential, so that you can keep track of what works – and why.

Of course, safety is paramount. With this in mind, some reminders:

* If you go foraging, do make sure you know for sure what plants you are collecting as some are toxic and should not be eaten or even handled.

* Avoid essential oils if you have any allergies.

* Incense and fire must be treated with caution. If you are in any doubt about lighting a candle, don't do it. Instead, imagine your candle is lit, practising visualisation to ensure that it is convincing.

Here are some points to consider when working on your own spells, to help you hone your craft.

Reflection

* What is your intention?

* What do you really want to manifest?

* What must you prioritise? Sort out what matters most to you right now and eliminate all maybes and ifs.

* Gather thoughts, gather feelings, then gather ingredients.

Practice

* Use what is in season; align your intentions with nature's energy and the local environment.

* Check out traditional timings about when it is good to cast spells, whether for love, success or anything else.

* Improvise, be creative and don't be fearful – if it sounds and looks how you want it to be, then it's right for you.

* Be open to your imagination and intuition.

* If you're not a solitary type, join in with other witchy people, or even a 'coven', if you feel so inclined.

Review

* Check in with yourself and your goals frequently.

* Get out in nature.

* Pick your moments.

* Keep a journal, diary or Book of Shadows.

USING WORDS IN SPELLS

Using incantations and mantras creates a powerful channel to the universe. Many spells use words because spelling out our desires – whether written, spoken, in rhyme or improvised – empowers our intentions with the magic of language.

In particular, by naming the elements, colours, directions, deities and so on in your spells, you will reinforce your intention – and the more you imbue your incantation with corresponding energies, the more likely it is that it will encourage the manifestation of your desire. Here are a few ideas to get you going:

The elements
'By Fire, and Water, Air and Earth . . .'
Or you can use the elements individually.

Colours
'With red, I ignite my intention to . . .'
'This blue attracts lunar light to help . . .'
'With yellow, I seek and discover . . .'
'Add green and nature rewards me . . .'

The four directions
'From south, the warm wind brings creative . . .'
'From west, the breeze heralds change for . . .'
'From east, the sun rises to show me . . .'
'From north, the ice melts to reveal . . .'

Empowering words that mean something to you
'This charm, it . . .'

'I cast a spell to . . .'
'I believe in . . .'
'I trust . . .'
'I am empowered by . . .'
'I affirm and . . .'

Deities

'Oh, spirit . . .'
'Earth Mother . . .'
'Great Goddess . . .'
'Horned God, Cernunnos . . .'
'God of the forest . . .'
'Goddess of joy . . .'
'Oh, magic moon goddess . . .'
'Dear Selene . . .'

Numbers

'Take one for joy . . .'
'Take two stones and hold them to my . . .'
'With three, I bind . . .'
'With four ribbons, I braid a petition . . .'
'Five times round I coil the twine and . . .'
'Six brings favours . . .'
'Seven stars twinkling for . . .'
'Eight knots are tied . . .'
'Nine to manifest . . .'

Thanks and blessings

'Thank you, universe . . .'
'To all the spirits, blessings for . . .'

'Thank you, goddess of the moon . . .'
'Thank you, Jupiter (/Mars/Venus, etc.) . . .'
'I give gratitude to . . .'

Simple affirmations
'I believe in . . .'
'This magic is . . .'
'I have this . . .'
'I love . . .'
'I trust . . .'
'I am . . .'

To end
Always finish with thanks, gratitude or a blessing. Or say: 'So mote it be'.

Let it go

When you have finished your spell, it's time to let it go. After all, the universe is there to do what has to be done, to bring you the desire you seek. So give thanks to nature, to Mother Earth, to the universe and, most of all, to yourself.

Remind yourself: I am special, unique, a child of the universe, and I deserve to have what I believe is right for me, just by virtue of being born on this planet.

CONCLUSION

End and Beginning

*Everything that is in the heavens, on Earth, and under the earth
is penetrated with connectedness, penetrated with relatedness.*
Hildegard of Bingen, German mystic

Rather like the wheel of the year, we are, in a way, back at the place we started from. We may be at the literal, physical end of this book – there may be only a few more pages to read – but this book hasn't ended yet. For it is just the first chapter of a volume as yet unwritten. A volume called *The Manifestation of Your Best Self*.

Whether you first opened this book in spring, summer, autumn or winter, you have hopefully enjoyed stepping on to a path that leads to the discovery of who you are, a belief in and connection to your inner witch.

Through this book, you have reawakened your gifts of intuition and self-understanding. You have discovered a wide range of witchy tools and ingredients, as well as how to align yourself with nature's cycles to feel a magical connection to the universe. For you *are* part of the cosmic dance – a modern witch, who is now ready to call on all that is within and without you to make your dreams come true.

Blessings to you – and most of all, let the light of the universe shine through you every day, as you walk along the pathway to your chosen destiny.

Correspondence List

The list below is by no means exhaustive, but it will give you a wide range of other ingredients (or 'correspondences') that you can use as substitutes for the ones used in this book. It is also a great resource to draw on when creating your own spells.

Spells for Ambition and Success

Crystals	Botanicals
Clear quartz	Oak
Red carnelian	Hazel
Aquamarine	Sunflower
Tiger's eye	Basil
Ruby	Marigold
Malachite	Bay
Black obsidian	Olive
Aventurine	Sage
Citrine	Willow

Essential oils

Cedarwood
Oud
Wild orange
Vetiver
Sandalwood

Colours

Red
Green
Gold
Black

Elements/planets

Fire
Earth
Air
Sun
Moon
Uranus
Saturn
Jupiter

Deities

Jupiter
Cernunnos
Apollo
Brigid
Zeus
Helios
Thor

Spells for Love and Romance

Crystals

Garnet
Magnetite
Rose quartz
Red carnelian
Ruby
Citrine
Rhodochrosite
Emerald
Rose opal
Pink tourmaline

Botanicals

Apple
Thyme
Basil
Rose
Jasmine

Lily
Lavender
Hazel
Silver birch
Mugwort
Mint
Verbena

Essential oils

Patchouli
Lotus
Rose
Ylang ylang
Mint
Jasmine

Colours

Red
White
Pink
Rose
Indigo

Elements/planets

Venus
Water
Earth
Air
Fire
Moon
Jupiter
Neptune

Deities

Aphrodite
Venus
Zeus
Freya
Selene
Triple Goddess
Hera
Eros
Aine

Spells for Abundance, Luck and Prosperity

Crystals

Citrine
Aventurine
Emerald
Malachite
Lodestone
Red carnelian
Yellow sapphire
Tiger's eye
Turquoise

Botanicals

Clover
Oak
Beech
Pine
Bergamot
Ginger
Chilli
Dandelion
Sage
Olive

Essential oils

Patchouli
Bergamot
Oud

Ginger
Mint
Sage

Colours

Black
Red
Blue
Green

Elements/planets

Air
Fire
Earth
Sun
Jupiter
Mars
Mercury
Pluto

Deities

Great Goddess
Selene
Ares
Fortuna
Ploutos
Hermes

Spells for Friends, Family and Protection

Crystals

Citrine
Moonstone
Black tourmaline
Black obsidian
Amethyst
Selenite
Opal
Clear quartz

Botanicals

Comfrey
Basil
Beech
Oak
Cinnamon
Cypress
Yellow roses
Chamomile
Hawthorn

Essential oils

Sandalwood
Frankincense
Cedarwood
Ginger

Mint
Wild orange

Colours

Blue
Black
Gold
Red
Orange
Yellow
White

Elements/planets

Earth
Water
Air
Moon
Venus
Saturn
Mercury

Deities

Vesta
Hestia
Artemis
Hera

279

Lares
Penates

Horned God
Great Goddess

Spells for Creativity, Inspiration and Adventure

Crystals

Turquoise
Citrine
Clear quartz
Peridot
Moonstone
Sunstone
Green aventurine
Aquamarine
Fluorite
Bloodstone
Carnelian
Red jasper

Botanicals

Pomegranate (or seeds)
Sunflower (or seeds)
Lavender
Rosemary
Sage
Peppermint leaves
Hazel
Aspen

Silver birch
Basil
Bay
Wild garlic

Essential oils

Clary sage
Bergamot
Wild orange
Jasmine
Peppermint
Clove
Frankincense
Cypress

Colours

Blue
Green
Red
Gold
Yellow

Elements/planets

Fire
Earth
Air
Sun
Mercury
Jupiter
Uranus
Neptune

Deities

Zeus
Hermes
The nine Greek Muses
Apollo
Athene
Dionysus
Cerridwen
Brigid
Danu

Glossary

Affirmation A positive declaration about your intention, desire, belief or goal, used to reinforce a ritual, spell or other way of manifesting that intention.

Aura An invisible energy field radiating from the bodies of all living things; said to be made up of an electromagnetic spectrum of colours, discernible by those who have the ability to perceive it.

Chakras In Eastern spiritual traditions, the seven main chakras (a Sanskrit word meaning 'wheel') are epicentres or spinning vortexes of energy, which revolve or spiral about and through our bodies. They can be likened to swing doors, through which universal energy flows into and out of us. It is believed they vibrate to the electromagnetic frequency of colours that radiate from the aura. The main ones are the crown, third-eye, throat, heart, solar-plexus, sacral and base (or root) chakras.

Coven A group or gathering of witches.

Deity A divine being, usually either masculine or feminine, but sometimes both, who is from a pantheon of many gods who appear in different polytheistic religions; or a pair of gods who appear in a duo-theistic religious system (Wicca, for example).

Divination The art of looking into the future by means of reading patterns, signs and symbols. This is best known in the context of tools such as horoscopes, tarot cards, palm-reading, tea leaf-reading and scrying (gazing into a crystal ball).

Equinox The equinoxes are when the sun is immediately over the equator, and therefore day and night are of equal (or almost equal) length over twenty-four hours across the world.

Folklore Myths, stories, practices and beliefs that have been handed down through specific cultural generations and which define and give shape to the culture in question.

Geopathic stress Any unwanted negative energy from the environment, such as underground water courses, overhead electricity pylons and other cables, high-rise buildings, ley lines, hidden plague pits or burial grounds, earthworks, geological faults and so on.

Grimoire A book of magic spells that often includes divination techniques, instructions for talismans and amulets and incantations for calling on spiritual entities. In the

1940s, Wiccan founder, Gerald Gardner, designated this 'the Book of Shadows'.

Intention A desire, goal or statement of that which you want to manifest.

Lunar phases Four main lunar phases are referred to in this book: the waxing moon, the full moon, the waning moon and the dark of the moon. Some witches also include more specific phases, such as gibbous moons, first- and last-quarter moons and so on, which can often be found in traditional gardening or seasonal almanacs.

Manifestation The realisation, fulfilment or tangible evidence of a goal.

Psyche The soul. The most innermost place of oneself, named after Psyche, Greek goddess of the soul, who was usually represented with butterfly wings.

Ritual A series of actions to bring about change or to reinforce one's intentions, desires and beliefs.

Sabbat A festival or celebration held at certain times in the Wiccan wheel of the year (see below), giving blessings or thanks to the sun, moon and Earth deities.

Smudging Burning sacred herbs (usually sage) to purify and cleanse a space of all forms of negative energy.

Solstice The winter and summer solstices indicate the point in time when the sun 'stands still' for a moment, reaching its highest or lowest point in the sky, thus marking either the longest or shortest hours of daylight. Depending on whether you're in the northern or southern hemisphere, this also signals the beginning of summer or winter, according to the astronomical year.

Spell A spell is made up of an incantation to connect to the magical forces in nature and the universe plus a combination of corresponding ingredients and/or symbolic actions to reinforce the initial intention.

Symbol Meaning 'throwing together', a symbol is a mark, sign or shape that has a specific underlying meaning. When cryptic and mysterious, it may be understood only by those in the know.

Talisman A symbol, sign, image or object (such as a crystal or piece of jewellery) thought to have magic power to protect the wearer or user from negative energy.

Wheel of the year The wheel of the year is both a neopagan and Wiccan calendar of the year, which revolves around the cyclical relationship between the sun as god and the Earth as goddess. The god 'dies' each autumn and is reborn at Yule, growing fertile in spring and uniting with the goddess in summer, only to fade away again in the autumn, thus repeating the never-ending cycle of birth, growth and death. This echoes the cycles of nature, as the old makes way for the new. Each sabbat (see above) represents a specific stage of this mythic cycle, and the balance of the archetypal energies of the feminine and masculine principles.

Further Reading

Raymond Buckland, *Buckland's Complete Book of Witchcraft (Llewellyn's Practical Magick)*

Scott Cunningham, *Wicca: A Guide for the Solitary Practitioner*

Owen Davies, *Grimoires: A History of Magic Books*

Mike Dooley, *Infinite Possibilities: The Art of Living Your Dreams*

Dr Wayne W. Dyer, *The Power of Intention: Learning to Co-create Your World Your Way*

Janet and Stewart Farrar, *A Witches' Bible: The Complete Witches' Handbook*

Gerald E. Gardner, *The Gardnerian Book of Shadows: The Complete Wicca Initiations and Pagan Ritual Lore*

Judy Hall, *Manifesting with Crystals: Attracting Abundance, Wellness & Happiness*

Esther and Jerry Hicks, *Ask and It is Given: Learning to Manifest Your Desires*

Napoleon Hill, *The Law of Success*

Michael Howard, *Modern Wicca: A History from Gardner to the Present*

Arin Murphy-Hiscock, *The Green Witch: Your Complete Guide to the Natural Magic of Herbs, Flowers, Essential Oils, and More*

Shawn Robbins and Charity Bedell, *Good Witch's Guide: A Modern-Day Wiccapedia of Magickal Ingredients and Spells*

Eckhart Tolle, *The Power of Now: A Guide to Spiritual Enlightenment*

Acknowledgments

I would like to thank everyone at Yellow Kite, Hodder & Stoughton and Hachette who were involved in manifesting this book, especially Carolyn Thorne and Daniela Ferrante for keeping me on target and Anne Newman for her editorial guidance. To manifest anything, we need the support and encouragement from not only friends and family but also our colleagues, so I am truly thankful for working with such a brilliant team. I am also most grateful to my daughter, Jessica Bartlett, for contributing her illustrations, 'hare' and 'basil plant' to the 'witch's brew'! Last, but not least, I thank you, the reader, for choosing this book to manifest the best of yourself.

About the Author

After studying at the Faculty of Astrological Studies in London, the UK, Sarah gained the Diploma in Psychological Astrology – an in-depth 3-year professional training programme cross-fertilised by the fields of astrology and depth, humanistic and transpersonal psychology. She has worked extensively in the media as astrologer for titles such as *Cosmopolitan* magazine (UK), *SHE, Spirit & Destiny* and the *London Evening Standard*, and appeared on UK TV and radio shows, including *Steve Wright in the Afternoon* on BBC Radio 2. Her mainstream mind-body-spirit books include the international bestsellers, *The Tarot Bible, The Little Book of Practical Magic* and *Secrets of the Universe in 100 Symbols*. Sarah currently practises astrology and other esoteric arts in the countryside.